Mel Bay Presents

Acoustic
FINGERSTYLE GUITAR WORKSHOP

by Richard Gilewitz

1 2 3 4 5 6 7 8 9 0

Visit us on the Web at www.melbay.com — E-mail us at email@melbay.com

Table of Contents

CD Contents

The CD with this book is to be used as a reference. Each track is titled so you can match the written practice exercises and picking patterns with audio portion. Some of the tunes are preceded by historical notes. "Mrs. Firecracker's Place" contains both historical and performance notes.

Track	Exercises
1	Arpeggio Exercise
2	Tremolo Exercise
	Picking Patterns (each example played twice)
3	Inside Rolls
4	Forward Rolls
5	Inside Rolls with Pair
6	Forward Rolls with Pairs
7	Pinch Patterns
8	Pinch Patterns with Pairs
9	Arpeggio Patterns
	Extra Patterns
10	Hammer-on's
11	With Bass Movement
12	With Pair
13	With Double Hammer-on
14	Pull-off's
15	With Bass Movement
16	With Pair
17	With Double Pull-off
	Patterns and Songs
18	"Echoing Gilewitz" Patterns
19	"Echoing Gilewitz" (excerpt from Echoing Wilderness")
20	"Maison Blanche" Patterns
21	"The Maison Blanche Exit Song"
22	"Mrs. Firecracker" Patterns
	Forward Roll Inside Roll
	Pinch Patterns Inside Roll
	Forward Roll Inside Roll
	Pinch Patterns Inside Roll
23	"Mrs. Firecracker's Place"
24	"Pre-dawn Mourning"
25	"Jamaicalina"
26	"Bilingual Fantasy" (with percussion by Gumbi Ortiz) from *Synapse Collapse*
27	"Gypsy Minor"/"Dirt to Dust"
	"Dirt to Dust" (with percussion by Gumbi Ortiz)
28	"Gypsy Minor"/"Dirt to Dust" from *Thumbsing*

Photo Credit: Tim Ward

Here's what folks are saying about Richard Gilewitz and his workshops

"Richard's clinics have always inspired our customers to continue playing and enjoying music." Brendan Jang, Tom Lee Music, Vancouver, British Columbia

"If Richard was not such an incredible musician, he could have a career in standup comedy. The audience loved his clinic!" Dan Cartwright, Kitsap Music, Bremerton, Washington

"Just wanted to send a belated Thanks for coming up to Nova Scotia for our Annual Guitar Show. Our customers were very impressed, and we managed to sell a couple of guitars from it. We certainly would like to see you next year." David Mingo, Mingo Music, Truro, Nova Scotia

"I was particularly impressed with his control of dynamics. Hope to have him again. Thanks."
J G Nixon, Instrumental Music. Ludington, Michigan

"That was the best an acoustic guitar has ever sounded in this room in fourteen years."
Kevin Johnson, Act 1 Music and Sound, Langley,British Columbia

"Richard held an extraordinarily captive audience of young and old alike, who all delighted in his musicianship and humor, a real treat for all who attended. Richard's performance resulted in us making new friends and customers and our acoustic guitar and accessory sales jumped immediately following the clinic. Possibly the best clinic we have ever sponsored at any of the five Tarpley Music Company locations." Tony Eisenbraun, Tarpley Music, Clovis, New Mexico

" I saw your incredible performance and workshop at St. John's music in Winnipeg on April 6th. I wanted to tell you that that performance has forever changed the way I listen to, approach and play the guitar. I learned so much from those two hours that I'm still stunned that I just happened to be at the right place at the right time as I had no idea who you were or that a workshop was scheduled! Your music is refreshing and so well constructed that I've become entranced by the magic you weave with a few steel strings. Meanwhile I am spreading the word about your amazing music. Hope you come by Winnipeg again soon."
Paul Bourget, Winnipeg, Manitoba

"The Richard Gilewitz clinic was a huge success. We anticipated 20-30 people and 80 showed up. We are still receiving comments today (the day after) - people thanking us for holding the clinic. It is the best promotion we have ever put on in the five years we have been here. Richard made it a VERY enjoyable evening for everyone. I can't express in words how great this clinic was."
Stan Kirby, Instrumental Music, Gaylord, Michigan

"Just a quick note about the Richard Gilewitz concert and clinic we had on February 3rd. Richard's amazing playing style and great sense of humor were a fantastic showcase for Tacoma Guitars with their outstanding tone and affordability. The guy that won the DM-9 was thrilled to death. The crowd of over 120 were mesmerized by Richard's playing and personable humor.
Thank You." Phil Feser and the guys at Nightlife Music, Mandan, North Dakota

"Richard excels in his entertainer/clinician role while performing some amazing pieces; we drew the largest crowd yet and had lots of interest in products during the breaks; many comments from customers who enjoyed the show."
Robert Greenly, Mundt Music, Longview, Texas

"I was at Tempo Music on Nov. 16th and thoroughly enjoyed your performance. It exposed me to the real possibilities of the instrument. You are a great guitarist!" Jim Behan, Hendersonville, North Carolina

"I've taught my daughter (now 20 years old) to play guitar and have been somewhat disappointed in her lack of ambition to learn more for the past 2-3 years. Your performance had her leaving the room with a renewed desire to pursue her instrument with a new passion for excellence. For that I am most grateful."
Ray Marquardt, Mankato, Minnesota

"Last Thursday night we packed over 80 people into our shop. Everyone was completely blown away!! Not only is Richard a truly amazing guitarist, he is incredibly funny and entertaining." Mark Horn, Bluer Music, Ooltewah, Tennessee

About the Author

Composing and performing a kaleidoscopic mixture of instrumental selections for the guitar, Richard Gilewitz is an internationally acclaimed solo performer who has forged a new voice to include the expanse of his influences. His complex and energetic original works become stories from the guitar and deliver invitations to each listener to take a journey with him through the past and present realm of guitar music.

As one of the most graceful fingerstyle guitarists on the contemporary acoustic scene, Gilewitz stands out in his command of the 6 and 12-string guitar. His right hand technique - a compilation of the classical guitar technique and syncopated percussive movements - enables Richard to vary his *attack* and create a wider range of tone and fingerpicking patterns as a *language*. Combining both standard and alternate tunings with his interpretations, every single note is treated as an individual character in a society of notes. Achieving a distinctive sound with a voice of its own, Richard jokes that his own *DNA* is reflected in his playing.

Richard began honing his skills both as a performer and composer during the late 1970's at the University of Alabama, playing the local coffeehouse circuit while pursuing degrees in Computer Science, Mathematics, and Music. Following graduation, he placed his music career in the background and joined the business world of flight simulation design, telemetry and satellite systems. Soon the pull of his passion for music was so compelling that Richard left corporate life to teach and perform full time.

The 1980's brought Richard to Florida where he released his first LP recording, *Somewhere In Between.* Since that time, he has traveled many miles as a favorite performer at festivals, colleges, performing arts centers, and intimate concert halls. He has released four recordings on compact disc *(Voluntary Solitary, Synapse Collapse, The Music of David Walbert,* and *Thumbsing);* an instructional guitar video titled *Music and Instruction for Fingerstyle Guitar,* and a songbook collection. Presently Richard is working with Mel Bay Publications on a number of other projects including a performance DVD, a book about the nylon and steel string guitar, and a contribution to the *Master Anthology of Fingerstyle Guitar Solos, Volume 3.*

Because teaching involves a major portion of Richard's touring schedule, he is in demand for his individual lessons, group Master Classes, and his popular Guitar Seminar Workshop Series. Many of these workshops are conducted on behalf of several major companies involved in the music industry. His *Meet the Artist - Music in the Schools Enrichment Program* ® gives Richard the opportunity to meet with elementary, middle school, and high school students for a one-day event or during a longer in-residence program that includes lessons and a final assembly with the students.

As a freelance writer, Richard has been published in Peavey Electronics' trade journal, *Monitor*, Disc Makers' *fastFORWARD*, Mel Bay Publications' on-line magazine, *Guitar Sessions*®, and in other trade and on-line magazines. Radio appearances include BBC Ireland, Radio New Zealand, RTE, *River City Folk*, *E-Town*, *Live from Studio One*, *WoodSongs Old Time Radio Hour*, *Across the Prairi*e, and *WUWF Radio Live!*.

Richard has appeared in concert with: John Renbourn, Mose Allison, John Fahey, Leo Kottke, Norman Blake, Kenny G, Adrian Legg, The Little River Band, David Bromberg, Taj Mahal, Greg Brown, John Hammond, Steve Morse, Patty Larkin, The Indigo Girls, Joe Ely, Rory Block, America, Mike Cross, Sonny Landreth, Maria Muldaur, Jane Siberry, and Jorma Kaukonen.

Chapter One: Why Write a Guitar Workshop Book?

I wanted to play drums originally. My parents found out about the idea and promptly bought me a guitar. My Mom said I could pick up girls at the beach with it, which was interesting since I was only 7 years old. I really didn't get serious about the guitar until around age 14 and have been playing ever since. At the time of the writing of this book, I have been playing about 31 years.

During the past ten years of conducting fingerstyle and sound reinforcement seminars in a variety of settings worldwide, I have had the opportunity to gather a wealth of useful material. These seminars have been included in the programs of college music departments, middle and high school enrichment classes, guitar workshop seminars, music society special classes, festivals, and in particular, music shops. In 2000-2001 alone, touring to 300 music dealers in 45 states in America and abroad to Canada, New Zealand, Wales, Ireland, and England, I have instructed students of all levels of achievement and playing style and have learned a great deal from them. Until recently, the crowd mostly consisted of males, giving me the impression that I had been conducting "Tupperware®" guitar parties for men! But lately, I have been encouraged by the enthusiasm not only from women, but also from people of all ages with such a widespread interest in musical styles. Acoustic fingerstyle guitar seems to have a common ground for everyone.

When first embarking on this journey, my intention was to keep things simple. I thought these sessions would entail just explaining my right hand picking style, giving some suggestions on the use of open tunings, and offering thoughts on composition. Much to my surprise, I was continuously challenged by the audience to address nuances I had not expected. Questions poured from students encompassing subjects about the depth of composition and the creative process involved and stumbling blocks to overcome. They asked how to address peaks and valleys during a lifetime of playing, how to amplify an acoustic guitar in a multitude of settings, and what a performer may experience with the vast array of equipment available in today's market.

What also surprised me was the majority of questions were absolutely consistent -regardless of the level of player I was teaching or the location of the seminar. Simple things such as fingernail care, fingerstyle patterns in the development of a right hand language, how often to practice and even how to practice were always topics of discussion.

This book is a summary of these workshops -- the questions, my feelings, answers, and suggestions while utilizing original compositions to help explain and simplify concepts. It is designed to benefit players of all age, level and style who have either attended one of my clinics, have missed the opportunity to attend or because of circumstances, have never had the opportunity. It can be used as a companion piece to the enclosed DVD, as well as during the seminar and afterwards as a review and refresher course. It can also be used by instructors teaching at colleges and universities, music shops, and in private settings.

Chapter Two addresses the five most frequently asked questions. These queries are then followed by a number of common, and not so common questions, which are answered and supported by written explanations, exercises, music tablature and notation pieces, charts, photographs, and drawings. A CD that demonstrates how each exercise and piece should sound is provided. Some of the topics include: open tunings, establishing a rhythmic groove in a piece, reasons why a particular guitar might be selected for a piece, the use of a capo, or how to adjust a metronome to discover where a piece of music really lives...and of course, fingernail care!

It is my intention to provide a useful book that kindles a desire to learn fingerstyle guitar. This book should encourage the player to begin or continue working on a life-long craft, offering answers to many questions and presenting new avenues for growth.

Chapter Two: Questions

Can we start with the five most frequently asked questions?

The following are the most common questions I am asked during my guitar workshops, regardless of region or population of the community where the seminar is held. These questions are always fascinating to me because they are usually asked just after I have played for the audience for approximately 45 minutes. Generally these first five questions have nothing to do with the acoustic guitar!

These questions are not necessarily in any order. Some of the answers are expanded upon in subsequent chapters.

1. Where are you from?
I was born in San Diego, California and grew up in New Jersey, Alabama, and Florida.

2. How long have you been playing?
I began playing as a 14 year-old in 1974. At the printing of this book, I have been playing the guitar 31 years.

3. Do you play electric guitar?
No, but I have one hanging on my wall. I never seemed drawn to play one, but I do enjoy listening to an electric guitar. I like the sound of an electric depending on the player and the music. So I won't rule it out for a future project.

4. Have you ever played in a band?
No. But I have had the good fortune of some great players joining in with me. Mostly I enjoy working with the sounds of a fiddle, piano, cello, or flute. For a real blast I like to play with a good percussionist for that extra driving rhythmic element.

5. Do you play any other instruments?
At one point earlier in my career I attempted playing the harmonica. A real harmonica player saw me in action one day and said, "Hey Gilewitz! Did you know if you breathe in you get all the other notes?!" Then he commented, "You could hold it out the car window while you're driving down the road and get what you're doing!"...

I was also once asked to contribute some licks on my Banjitar for a portion of the soundtrack to an independent film some friends of mine were making in St. Louis, MO. The Banjitar is an instrument that has six strings and is played like a guitar but has the resonator body of a banjo. I agreed to provide some music as long as they would create a role in the film for me. They did. I am Agent Cupcake and the film is entitled *Inbred Redneck Alien Abduction.* (There is a little part of me that hopes it is never released!)

I do play a classical (or nylon string) guitar, and have several 6 and 12-steel string guitars. That's it for right now.

Chapter Three: Selecting a Guitar

How do you select a guitar?

When selecting a guitar I almost treat the venture similarly to writing a tune. I tend to let the guitar *find me.* Much like my composing, which is done through trial and error, I often think of it as *reverse fishing* where the fish catches you! In other words, I take my time and play several guitars. Through the process of elimination I eventually whittle down the competition to one or two. (Yes, you can have two!) I have about 14 instruments now, including four 12-strings, seven 6-strings, a classical, an electric and a *Banjitar* which is a 6-string banjo tuned and played like a guitar. You have to decide for yourself about the guitar that suits your taste. It depends on your body and hand size, types of wood for a particular tone, string selection, and preferred action (height of the strings from the fingerboard).

Photo Credit: Wayne Brown

I generally gravitate toward a lower action since I don't want my left hand working too hard; it also facilitates left-hand speed and mobility. A lower action relaxes the general tension, thus reducing string resistance for my right-hand fingerpicking style. When *touring* through guitar rooms I personally enjoy either the longer sustain sound of a rosewood instrument or the low-end *thunk* of a mahogany guitar. I also have heard that *monogamy* guitars are nice, but tend to separate after five years. Just kidding!

Remember, like a new shoe, some guitars are built to break in after a time. I have heard of some classical guitarists who, prior to concertizing, place their new instrument in front of a speaker in their home or studio. The theory is that the music playing into the soundhole for some amount of time causes the guitar to resonate and *break in* sooner.

Chapter Four: The 12-String Guitar

Can you tell me about the 12-string guitar? Explain just how you tune it, and explain why you tune it so low.

When tuning my 12-string guitar I generally like to have an electronic tuner available. I use the tuner to establish a reference tone on string 1 and later as a checking device. In between, however, I switch off the tuner so that I can continue to train my intuition and ear, which can be neglected when relying exclusively on a tuner.

Photo Credit: Wayne Brown

I prefer to tune the 12-string down at least one whole step from standard tuning, often 1-1/2 steps or even 2 full steps lower, depending on the instrument's action (the distance of the strings from the guitar fingerboard). This reduces tension on the neck. I also feel that a 12-string is a more powerful rhythmic instrument and roars better when pitched down. In standard tuning, the strings are tuned from low to high: E A D G B E. If lowered one whole step, the notes would register on the tuner as: D G C F A D. Remember too, the first two pairs of strings (courses) are tuned in unison (same pitch) while courses 3 through 6 are tuned in octaves. The octave strings are exactly that --OCTAVE strings. So, if the larger string in the third course is a G, then the little string in the pair is also a G an octave higher (or in the whole-step, pitched-down tuning, both strings in the third course would be F's).

In my method of tuning the 12-string, I begin with the first and second courses of unison strings, using the tuner to establish the first note as a reference point. I then follow with course 3 on up to 6, checking the low string in each course with either a matched unison or octave string on one of the higher strings. For example, once I have courses 1 and 2 tuned and I am ready to check the 3rd course, I check the open G against the 1st string fingered at the 3rd fret. Then I'll match the 3rd string, 4th fret against the 2nd string open (comparing B's as in the normal 6-string tuning process). Keep in mind my explanation uses note names that assume we are not pitched down a whole tone. Once the low third string is in tune, I match its octave counterpart and continue similarly through course 6.

Once you have completed this process, start all over again to fine-tune the guitar. You may also wish to use the harmonic tuning method (using harmonics at frets 5, 7, and 12) and octave harmonics to compare both open and fretted notes. For example, check the octave harmonic on the low 4th course D with the open octave (high) D, the D on the second string, third fret, and the third string 7th fret (all D's)- checking both pairs of strings and cross-string relationships. Remember that guitars go out of tune for a living, especially if your strings are new! With new strings, you may want to run your left-hand index finger along the string from fret 1 to 12 while pulling the string slightly away from the guitar with your right hand. This will help stretch the string uniformly and make tuning easier, allowing a new string to stabilize sooner and insuring that the strings are appropriately taut on the tuning post and locked in place at the ball end under the bridge pin.

Photo Credit: Richard Gilewitz

Check the tuning of the instrument intuitively by testing very slowly with a few full and partial chords (the D chord, for example, or ADF♯ on courses 3, 2 and 1). Take your time, and listen. Use your electronic tuner at this point to check everything. If your intuitive tuning doesn't agree with the electronic tuner, you may want to have the instrument's intonation examined by a luthier.

Lately, I have been using D'Addario EXP 80/20 or Phosphor Bronze strings, which work well with both magnetic or piezo pickups. I generally use a light gauge set ranging from 12-53 with an 11 for the 3rd course octave, 16 for the 4th octave, 22 WOUND! for the 5th course octave, and 30 wound for the 6th octave. As a fingerstyle player, I've found that an unwound fifth course octave string tends to dominate the entire low end, negating the low-end growl so desirable on a 12-string. Currently I'm using an external Audio-Technica AT4041 condenser mic (placed one foot in front of the sound hole on a boom stand) in conjunction with an L.R. Baggs M1 magnetic pickup.

Many ancient and modern instruments feature pairs of strings but relatively few are tuned in octaves like the 12-string guitar. The Baroque lute featured up to fourteen courses; the first course consisted of a single string as it frequently carried the melody or was responsible for ornamented fast passages. The Spanish vijuela, a seventeenth century predecessor to the modern guitar, had five pairs of strings tuned in unison. The entire mandolin family (mandolin, mandola, mandocello) uses four pairs of strings tuned in unison.

(The last contributed by Stephen Rekas of Mel Bay Publications. Many thanks!)

Chapter Five: String Gauges/Options

What about the string gauge for all your other guitars?

Because the action is set fairly low on my 6-string guitar and so I don't feel as if I'm playing with an emergency brake on, I use a light gauge set (12 16 24 32 42 53).

I pitch the 12-string guitar down two whole steps from standard and often use an open G tuning, which actually drops the low bass down to a B♭ (sounds great through a subwoofer!). Once again, the action is still fairly low and, due to the deeper tuning, I'll use the gauges in pairs as follows (the unisons on strings 1 and 2 and octaves on strings 3 through 6 are listed respectively): 13/13, 16/16, 24/11, 32/16, 42/22 wound, 56/30 wound. The real key here for me is the 5th string octave as a wound string. As a fingerstyle player the last thing I want to hear, when I come down with my thumb on the 5th string, is an unwound and amplified string.

Experiment with different types of strings. There are many string compositions available to suit your personal taste including bright bronze, golden bronze, phosphor bronze, white bronze, vintage bronze, flat-wound, and silk and steel. Some strings with a heavier nickel composition respond particularly well with a magnetic pickup. See what sounds good to your ear and how they feel under your fingers. Notice the effect of certain string qualities with different guitars as well as the effect they have on the different types of pieces in your repertoire. Also, see how they react to different types of pickup systems or microphones if you are performing, recording or just playing through a sound system for yourself. Become familiar with the life of the strings and be sure to get in the habit of changing them so you can maintain your level of inspiration.

Chapter Six: Capos

Why do you use a capo on your guitar if you don't sing?
What do you mean by 'where a tune lives'?

Obviously, a piece of music that might be performed on different instruments, such as a 6-string (steel-string), 12-string or nylon-string (classical) guitar, will take on different *flavors*. Just as a piece is either learned or created, there is a tendency to develop a preference towards one or the other of these instruments. For example, a melodic piece may find its way more easily onto a classical guitar, whereas a more thunderous and rhythmic slide piece would be ideal for the 12-string and thoroughly inappropriate on the classical.

Additionally, a player may find that a capo on the fourth fret will allow a piece to easily sustain a group of tones in a more desirable fashion as well as allow for ease of fingering. For example, I had once a piece of music which did not fit the 12-string until I used a capo on the fifth fret creating a harpsichord-like effect, which was actually what I had been hearing in my head while composing.

Another crucial factor is the use of a metronome or drum machine - not only for the actual timing of the piece, but as a tempo locator. In other words, you may find a piece can be played at a setting of 72 all the way up to 96 on your metronome. Eventually you may establish a *comfort zone*, which may vary over time depending on some surprising elements, such as your confidence in the tune or how much sleep you have had! During a live performance you may find yourself playing a selection faster, and that is when you have to ask yourself if the tune really belongs there or if you have just subjected not only yourself but your audience to a mild anxiety attack! You will find that if you trust the pocket where you have found the music to live, your musicianship as well as live performances will be a great deal more effective.

An example of one piece of music I have written demonstrating this concept is "Mrs. Firecracker's Place". Over time I experimented with the *groove* of the piece and the nature of the music. I wanted to let the tune *ride along* so to speak. I eventually tried to get my opinion out of the way and allow the tune to *let me know* where it wanted to be. I also discovered that a capo on the second fret created a lengthier blend of the tones, which allowed for a smoother undercurrent.

Photo Credit: Wayne Brown

Chapter Seven: Slide and Techniques for Playing Slide

Can you tell us what type of slide you are using, something about your slide playing techniques, and if you always play with the guitar in open tuning?

Photo Credit: Wayne Brown

I have used many slides and one of my favorites has been the *AcoustaGlide*, manufactured by a company out of Minnesota called Latch Lake. Guitarist Leo Kottke was involved in the development of this slide. I also use the Martin Simpson slide by Planet Waves. There are many choices of slide. Some are glass, some are ceramic, and some are brass. I have always preferred a thicker, heavier slide for better tone.

I wear the slide on my left pinkie so that I am free to chord with the remaining three fingers. I treat the entire left hand as a single group as I keep all the fingers (including the slide) close together. I try to be sure my entire left hand is also very relaxed. Good slide playing comes from fluidity. The left-hand ring finger braces against the slide, the middle finger arches up slightly mainly to get out of the way, and most importantly the left-hand index finger *lightly* touches the strings to *dampen* them. This allows for a smooth tone for your slide sound. Occasionally I will purposely lift the index finger off the strings and get a desired *rattle*. Be careful not to do this too often or your slide playing may sound like a bag of cats! When damping behind the slide be sure to cover only the exact number of strings the slide is covering.

I play slide exclusively in open tuning but I understand many lead guitarists, especially electric, lap steel, and Dobro® players, can be very effective with single-note slide play in standard and other tunings.

Chapter Eight: Practice Routine

Do you have a practice routine?

When I first began playing guitar I had to *will* myself to practice. I was not very good; learning was a slow and difficult process for me and it seemed initially like more work than fun. Fortunately, I stuck with it and by the time I was mid-way through high school I had a few tunes, some technique and a little bit of theory under my belt. At that point with somewhat of a foundation, I set up a schedule or at least marked down how long and *what* I had practiced.

In college at the University of Alabama I had a different approach. I decided to always keep my guitars out of the cases, in different tunings, and always well within reach. I would force myself to pick one of them up and if I didn't feel like playing I didn't hesitate to simply put it down. I placed myself in an environment and created a mindset that playing should be fun. As a result, I picked them up often and I was always focused on both good technique and repertoire additions.

I still firmly believe that always working with an existing new piece of music for the repertoire, revising an old tune or developing a new *original* piece is crucial in keeping the interest in the instrument. Also, further studies branching away from the guitar such as an indulgence or at least *exposure* to other art forms is good for the steady diet of your general musicianship.

At this time, guitar playing and music in general seem to be a huge part of my life and indulgence is natural. Playing guitar on and off throughout the day, or even taking a break for a couple of days also feels natural. At times I have to remind myself to do other things since if (I am indulging too much) I can feel out of balance, which in the long run can hurt the music. I feel the important thing is to not take it all so seriously, or that will come out in a performance. I also believe, however, that hard work, perseverance, and long-term dedication almost guarantee a payoff.

Chapter Nine: Burnout, Inspiration, and Rekindling

What inspires you to write or simply practice?
How do you maintain your enthusiasm for the guitar?

There are many areas to address when attempting to trigger the desire to play. Not specifically in any order, these are some of the thoughts I have that currently come to mind.

Be sure that your instrument is desirable to play. Check the action (height of the strings from the fingerboard) and determine whether or not it is too difficult to play. If it is too difficult to press down the notes and chords, then take the time to have your saddle adjusted, the nut filed, or the truss rod in the neck adjusted in the neck to make the instrument more playable. Also, have your local luthier check the intonation of the guitar. It is possible that either further *tweaking* is required or it may be time for you to consider upgrading to a new instrument.

Try putting fresh strings on the guitar and use a chromatic tuner to continuously recheck the tuning. Running your left-hand index finger along the fretboard on each string while simultaneously pulling the string slightly away from the guitar with your right hand, tends to help stretch new strings and helps them stay in tune sooner. Sometimes just the sound of new strings can provide the spark that is needed to get you practicing again.

Work with a new piece of music so that you always have a project in which you can indulge. One of my teachers recommended the following approach to a new piece. He suggested I simply attempt to play through the entire piece very slowly to see what I was up against. After a few passes through, repeated patterns, phrases, and subtle changes and nuances become more recognizable. At that point, the piece becomes less intimidating.

Try making some *stuff* up. Simply put, that is what you can try and do. Or as I've always said, *not try*. After an extended session of trial and error, fooling around, and attempting things that shouldn't work, little ideas will start to form. For me, they almost always show up as a sort of sucker punch. After playing for a long period of time with nothing happening, I disconnect and right about the time the drool shows up, so does the little motif, phrase or fragment of an idea.

Also, you must have a willingness to wait along with an acceptance of the peaks and valleys. I have spoken with many great players who have agreed that ups and downs, dry periods, and writer's block all exist, and that part of the process is accepting the fact that sometimes the spark isn't there. The music doesn't *show up*, and the waiting periods are simply a part of the process. This by no means suggests that you shouldn't play during these periods. More than any other time, it is best to play through these dry spells as eventually, something will happen. Sometimes I have purposely *not played* for a few days, even if I wanted to pick up the instrument. Some of this might be stubbornness on my part but it also allows for a certain buildup to occur. By the time I would finally give myself *permission* to play, I had such a craving that all kinds of ideas would pop up. The desire and spark was back. For some this might be a dangerous proposal since it just might be this approach that convinces someone to put the instrument down, and keep it down. Beware!

Another approach to avoid this risk of completely losing interest is to pick up the guitar several times throughout the day, play a little bit and then, even if you have the *desire* to play, force yourself to put it down. This is another approach I have used to regain that craving.

Lastly (but not *lastly*), attend concerts and music seminars, watch instructional videos, involve yourself with a local coffeehouse or open-mic night series in your town, seek out fellow musicians who like to get together to play and share ideas, and work with a good teacher. Part of the teacher's job should be to discover something about you as a student and provide some music for you to work on and rekindle the interest.

Chapter Ten: Influences

Can you tell us about your influences and where your music comes from?

I remember as a little kid listening to Burl Ives records and then, out of the blue one day, my dad brought home the Beatles album *Help!* I was never the same. To this day I am still a huge Beatles fan and have always admired the band's depth of character, growth and the pure joy and emotion they created in their music.

In my youth my parents also used to take the family to Renfro Valley, Kentucky for the annual Bluegrass Festival. The sounds I heard and the environment in general had a profound effect on my early musical aspirations.

As a teenager I was exposed to the playing of Arlo Guthrie's "Alice's Restaurant", Donovan's "Hurdy Gurdy Man", and the banjo playing licks from "Foggy Mountain Breakdown" featured in the film *Bonnie and Clyde.* At this point I became attracted to the guitar, particularly fingerstyle since it most closely resembled a banjo style.

I also soaked up the influences of all the music I heard on the *Dr. Demento Radio Show* and Wolfman Jack's *Midnight Special.* It was at this point, during the mid-70s, that my cousin introduced me to the guitar music of John Fahey, Leo Kottke, and Peter Lang. I still consider the music of these three players to be the most profound foundation for my current styling along with David Walbert, my classical guitar instructor and friend for nearly twenty years.

Photo Credit: Wayne Brown

I met David at the University of Alabama in the late 70s and his inspiration and eccentricity has had an undercurrent in my musical psyche ever since. "Why didn't you hold the melody?!". "What are you doing with THAT note?!!". Rumor has it Dave even pulled an ice pick out on a student once and started jabbing at his right hand. Years later I had the nerve to ask David about this and he simply shrugged and replied, "Well, you should have seen how high his thumb was!" All that said, I still owe the world to David for his patient, imaginative, and unparalleled instruction.

As far as the music I listen or listened to, I can list just about everything. Here is a short, diverse, and undefended list not in any particular order.

The Beatles, ABBA, U2, Fleetwood Mac, The Doobie Brothers, Elton John, Cat Stevens, Jim Croce, Enya, Depeche Mode, Kraftwerk, J. S. Bach, Andres Segovia, John Williams, Christopher Parkening, John Hammond, Doc Watson, Sonny Landreth, Leo Kottke, John Fahey, Peter Lang, David Walbert, and The Beatles (yes, they were that good).

Chapter Eleven: Composing

Do you prefer composing or learning/interpreting pieces of music written by others?

I enjoy both since I see value in each endeavor. Composing is a way of expressing your own voice in music and is an achievement in acknowledging the collective influences of your musical inspirations. Learning existing pieces is also a pleasure since it is a real treat to gain control of music you admire, getting it *under your fingers* and seeing how you choose to interpret the themes and melodies. Regardless of the music being original or interpreted, it is still essentially your *DNA* you are putting into the treatment of the tune. I am convinced that no two people play the same piece exactly alike.

Studying with David Walbert

When I compose I use that reverse fishing idea: the more research you have done about various styles of music, the more you study theory, and the more you get with other players to talk or jam, the better *bait* you'll wind up with when searching for tunes. It is almost like the sky scanning approach used by Jodie Foster's character in the movie "Contact". She knew there was something out there and just had to look in a lot of *space* to find it.

Writing is hard, but it can be done. Wait. Play. Disconnect. Look for rhythm, groove, melody, or motif to kick start your idea. Think about the melodies or rhythms away from the instrument allowing yourself to become *hungry* to create. Write in your head *away* from the guitar. Run the melodies, rhythms, and groove for particular tunes through yourself throughout the day. Listen to other instruments and styles; think of things unrelated to music that are inspiring and try to *relocate* that inspiration on your instrument.

There are many avenues to help you work the tune, such as a call and response or other traditional forms, grace notes, the use of dynamics, and space. Consider timing when composing by including rhythmic interruptions and syncopation. Be sure not to just *shock* the listener. Be effective. Familiarize yourself with these concepts in music. Have fun fiddling around and don't be afraid of trial and error. By the use of restraint, you can begin to sense the undercurrents in your music and allow them to cruise within the tune. Let the tunes grow up and evolve over time. I may work on a new tune and then *put it in the attic* for a time, allowing it to grow up. I also play new pieces *currently under construction* in a live setting. Many times I find that the adjustments I make during a live performance add to the tune, forcing me to drop the fear of moving sections around or improvising *within the tunes*. Sometimes I will select a piece to be recorded or performed on a 6-string or 12-string guitar, depending on where the tune seems to *live* more comfortably.

Improvise *within* the note. See how many different ways you can characterize each individual note in a piece along with its path to the next note. The Beatles have always been a big influence on me since so many of their tunes had such individual character, such an identifiable voice and mood of their own.

Work with vibrato, staccato, mutes, bends, hammer-ons, pull-offs, trills, rubato, legato, and the overall rhythmic feel of a tune. Also, understand intuitively *why* you selected a certain treatment of the note out of all the choices available to you. This will allow you to flavor and 'color' the music more. Experiment with leaving notes out...giving the composition room to breathe and the listener that instantaneous wonderment of where, when and how you will return to the theme.

Although brief, this last technique can be one of the most effective: Compose in the dark.

Chapter Twelve: Education Background

Can you tell us about your education and how it played a role in both your early years of development, and how you got into touring and recording? Also, are you still continuing your education?

My first guitar teacher in Huntsville, Alabama in the mid-1970s played a key role in my initial development as a practitioner of the instrument. It was Stan Lee's patience, methods, and direction that gave me a foundation to at least have a chance to continue. In other words, your teachers and mentors in the initial learning stages are key factors in your development as a player and determining whether you will continue to learn your instrument.

While at Grissom High School in Huntsville, I also enrolled in a music theory class that was taught by the school band teacher. My initial studies included key signatures, chord development, phrasing, and consideration of other instruments during the composition process.

My music theory education continued at the University of Alabama in the late 1970s as I studied for my degrees in Computer Science, Math, and Music. Building on what I had learned in high school, I studied ear training, composition, interval recognition, and the history of both obscure and well-known composers.

I first met David Walbert in 1978 at the University of Alabama, at the urging of a college dorm friend, Alex Ulloa. I remember Alex's wild-eyed look when he said, "You've got to try to sign up to study with this guy. He's the best I've ever heard!" Lucky for me David had one space open in his busy schedule. Not only did he travel to Tuscaloosa to teach at the University, but he was also part-owner of a guitar shop in Birmingham, an hour away.

During my lessons, David was inspired (for reasons beyond me) to nickname me in the fashion of the legendary blues player, Blind Lemon Jefferson. According to David I was to be named after an affliction, a fruit, and a president's last name. So my nickname for the semester was "Leper Banana Nixon". Dave also once proclaimed that I tended to, "make a face like a cat in a litter box" while playing. He suggested I practice smiling while I played. I eventually could not turn it off and he then commented that I was the only person or student he's ever seen who could smile while playing in a minor key.

Following that semester, I made several trips to Birmingham for more lessons as David had discontinued teaching at the University. Soon afterwards, he ventured to Spain and for a brief period, we lost touch. A few years later, upon returning to the States, he contacted me prior to his moving to Longboat Key, Florida where we developed a friendship and I continued my studies.

About this time, David began an affiliation with the inventors of the well-known board game *Trivial Pursuit* and he became the only American writer for the game. It was also during this period that I realized David had written some wonderful pieces of music for the guitar. It was not until the mid- to late 1990's that I was able to obtain all of these pieces and consider recording them.

On a self-titled LP recorded in 1980, David had released "Study", "Prelude", and "Dance". I have since re-recorded "Study" and "Prelude" on my first CD, *Voluntary Solitary* and "Dance" and "Prelude No. 2" on my second CD *Synapse Collapse*. The CD, *The Music of David Walbert*, contains all of these pieces as recorded during the summer of 2000. Although all of these tunes were written on a classical (or nylon-string) guitar, I have adapted them to the steel-string guitar since this is the instrument I have become most comfortable with during my years of recording, touring, and performing.

Other notes of interest: I taught David to type and after three weeks of diligent practice he was typing 12 words per minute with 32 percent accuracy. That same semester he gave me a 'B' in my guitar class. It was also during these years at the University of Alabama (from 1977-81) that I began performing in the local coffeehouse and eventually shared management duties with a friend. Some of my fondest and most *embarrassing* moments occurred during this period of my development as a musician, so I always encourage people to get out and play their music. There is something you get from performing which can't be *absorbed* into your musical being in any other way.

When I moved to Tampa, Florida in the early 1980s, following this period of school coffeehouse performances, I began performing at open-mic nights, restaurant gigs, small music venues, and eventually as an opening act for name touring artists. It was after this time that I began touring and working with company sponsors and regional sales representatives. Meeting soundmen, studio engineers, and my own involvement in recording studios still continues to play a role in my education. I continue to study with David Walbert whenever possible. He once asked me *over the telephone* as I played him a fragment of a piece, why I used my middle finger instead of my ring finger to strike a string. He also continues to beat the socks off of me in tennis.

You never stop learning. I feel that every class I attended in high school and college added to my musical development, whether it was calculus, physics, computers, English composition or a foreign language. Other endeavors and hobbies from building model rockets to martial arts have played a role in my education and development as a musician. From these interests I have learned the importance of detail, focus, respect, discipline, confidence, perfection, and acceptance.

Photo Credit: Wayne Brown

Chapter Thirteen: Amplification of an Acoustic Guitar

How do you amplify your guitars?

When amplifying an acoustic guitar there are a number of variables to consider: the style of pickup being used, microphones, the type of instrument, solo or band setting, string gauges and options, sound equipment available, player attack, expected crowd capacity, room conditions, and communicating with either a house or hired soundman.

Pickups

There are a variety of pickups available, including saddle or *piezo* pickups (some offering an internal microphone combination) and magnetic soundhole pickups. Some of these pickups are *passive*, which generally requires some sort of a pre-amp or 'boost' for the signal, and some pickups are *active*. Also, educate yourself about when a battery is required, when phantom power can be utilized, and when phantom power can cause problems.

For example, from time to time I am in a situation where the active magnetic pickup I have chosen can't utilize phantom power (risking damage to the pickup). But, I like to use an external condenser microphone which requires phantom power. I circumvent the situation by either switching pickups, switching to a mic that doesn't require phantom power, or going with a pickup-only sound. On rare occasions I may try the mic only for a smaller room, but I have always enjoyed the tones available from a good pickup.

Currently, I am using an L.R. Baggs M1 magnetic pickup system which is passive. I enjoy the option of adjusting the pole pieces for each string for a more controlled and balanced sound. I have also used, from time to time, a Fishman Rare Earth Double Coil magnetic pickup, which is an active pickup or a passive Sunrise magnetic pickup. Occasionally, I have been asked to demo an acoustic guitar with a built-in saddle pickup and there is often an option 'on-board' the guitar for some equalization and volume control. As I mention in the guitar and sound seminars I conduct, the choice of pickup really amounts to a matter of taste and a player's particular style.

Concerning the microphones of choice, realize that an external mic can be placed in a variety of positions. Also, when recording in a studio, the selection of mic placement is often different than in a live setting. There is an abundance of information on the variety of mics available. Do your own research, read the literature, and speak with engineers and soundmen in your quest for the right microphone.

Instruments

There are options to consider when amplifying the sound of your guitar, based on the instrument you will be playing. Often, this is determined by a matter of taste and the setting of the instrument. For example, I do not perform in a group setting. However, when I have heard a bluegrass guitarist in a band, I enjoy the sparkling tones that shimmer through with the use of a piezo pickup and/or microphone. The rest of the group rounds out the sound with plenty of bottom end and fill. As a listener in this setting, I do not think I would prefer the sound of a magnetic pickup. When listening to a classical guitarist, with good technique, I prefer an un-amplified instrument in a nice hall, or possibly adding a mic. With my 12- string guitar, I prefer mixing the M1 with a condenser mic and hope there is not a problem with too much phase cancellation.

Sound Equipment

This subject can take up to a zillion pages! There are many options to choose from and, if you are a touring artist, they will sometimes choose you. Even if you have particular requests in your contract rider, when you arrive at a venue you must be reasonably diplomatic and utilize whatever the house can provide. The best thing for ease of a sound check and zoning in on "your" sound is to educate yourself with the operation of as many different models and types of equipment as possible.

Power amps, equalizers, crossovers, subwoofers, a variety of 15" and 12" speakers, horn types, cone types, compressors, special effect units, and mixing consoles should all be a part of your study diet. You can obtain a great deal of information by visiting any music dealer that carries a variety of manufacturers' equipment from which to choose. Speaking with several trained sound and recording engineers to discuss functionality, as well as philosophies is a great way to enhance your knowledge of sound. More often than not they are willing and encouraged by your interest. Remember, they are artists too! There are schools for this training, but a tremendous amount of information is available for the simply curious individual.

When amplifying an acoustic guitar be sure to select the right pre-amp or D.I. (Direct Input) box for use with your particular pickup. Three of my favorites lately are the L.R. Baggs Para-Acoustic, the Brooks Siren, and the SansAmp, two of which have parametric capabilities. This allows me to adjust my midrange sweep control. Study gain structure as much as you can in order to properly use whatever equipment is available to you.

The following are some guitar frequencies you may want to consider when setting equalization for the room. Be aware that there are octaves to consider too such as 500 and 1K being octaves of 250 for example. I find that trouble areas for the guitar tend to occur around 125Hz, 500hz, 1k and 3k, especially the 500 which on an acoustic guitar tends to create that hollow or 'honk' sound. Also, I often pull the midrange out at least 3db (decibels) on the guitar's mixer channel. Just as you train your ear to recognize tunings and intervals, you should train your ear with the many sound systems and environments you find yourself working with from venue to venue. Unfortunately there really is no cut and dry formula to this process.

	Guitar Frequencies	
E2	80.2 Hz	(Hertz)
A2	107.0Hz	
D3	146.8Hz	
G3	195.2Hz	
B3	246.4Hz	
E4	328.5Hz	

Player attack

Remember, that all too often during a sound check, there is a certain feeling you may succumb to when you say to yourself, "Hey, there is nobody in the room"...and then, when the place fills up, your playing 'attack' completely changes. Be wary of this. If you suddenly play with a totally different 'fervor' during your show and overstrike your instrument, you may risk greatly affecting all that time you spent earlier conducting your sound check. While doing your sound check try to keep in mind how you expect to be playing during the show; more importantly, during the show, remember how you were playing during the sound check. I tend to sit out in the room in front of the speakers so I can hear my house sound, then I move onstage where we check the mics. I use very little monitor if at all.

Crowd Capacity/Room Conditions

The capacity of a room can also affect your sound check. This is often a cause for concern and depends on a variety of elements, including your sound equipment and the qualities in the room. To quote my sound engineer, "Everything affects everything." Some rooms have tile, wood, marble, or carpet. Some have high ceilings or metal ceilings; some are long or wide and have mirrors, glass ... and people, sometimes with winter coats!

Each of these factors can play a part in the final sound achieved during the show. Sound waves get baffled, bounced around, absorbed... you name it! Generally, I have noticed that a good-size crowd in a smaller room will 'soak up' the sound. So, I tend to run my (empty room) sound check a little hotter with a bit more bottom end and highs because I know that during the show, conditions may change. As an end result for a room, I prefer a sound that is full and balanced and not just LOUD. Oftentimes a good soundman is there for exactly that reason-- to make adjustments as needed. "Ah, that couple took off their jackets... I better change THIS!!".

Soundman Communication

On arriving at the venue, one of three things will occur concerning the sound person: you brought your own, you're going to be doing your own, or there is a house soundman. You may also have brought your own equipment or at least some of your own such as D.I. boxes, pre-amps, etc. During my sound checks, I always check the settings of the Pad and Low Cut buttons on the mixing console's individual channels. I tend to leave them disengaged or in the "off" position to avoid masking or disintegrating all of my bottom-end sound. I prefer to treat the acoustic guitar as a full-range instrument. The main objective is to always be professional, understand the sound you prefer and methods of obtaining that sound, and, most importantly, know how to communicate this concept to someone who may have never heard you play.

Unfortunately, the potential for confrontation is always there. When either the act has an attitude about what they're after and shows no respect for the soundman's knowledge and abilities, or vice versa, when the soundman disrespects the player, assuming that they don't know what they're talking about -- feathers get ruffled. I always attempt to communicate with the soundman on arrival with respect and professionalism. We are on the same team and the night is *ours* and not just mine. More times than not, a good soundman will respond with mutual respect, especially if you are honest with them. Minimally, you should have good command of your own equipment, its functionality, and know its negative tendancies. Observe what the sound company or house equipment entails, and then, let them do their job! After they have gotten 'a sound' for the room, if you are dissatisfied, offer some suggestions and inform them of the sound you want and adjustments you are making.

Once the show starts, the last thing you want to worry about is your sound. Your job at that point is to play and have fun. Oh, and always carry extra strings, batteries, cables, and cough drops!

###

Over the last ten years, I have had the pleasure of exclusively recording with George Harris at Panda Productions in Clearwater, Florida and Wayne Brown at Greenbrier Music in Anniston, Alabama. During the process of recording four separate CD projects, I have always found George and Wayne to be extremely knowledgeable. George has been kind enough to share his thoughts:

> "You could do a little more in the way of describing "phase" cancellation between a microphone and a pickup. One suggestion is to carry a "phase reverse" mic cable, for situations where the mixer does not have "phase" switches (these really reverse *polarity*). These cables are wired to reverse pins 2 & 3, and may have to be custom made). I have often found that reversing the polarity (phase) of the microphone yields a more useable blend. As you mentioned, this will take some degree of experimenting. You might also mention the possibility of bringing a reference CD to play for an unknown sound-person. Often this can be a large help in defining terms like "bright", or "full", etc..." George Harris, Panda Productions

Reprinted in part from Mel Bay Publications *Guitar Sessions®* article "Amplification of an Acoustic Guitar" by Richard Gilewitz, October 2001

Chapter Fourteen: What Is It Like to Perform Live?

Can you give us some tips on performing?

I can only tell you about my personal experiences and history more than actually telling anyone how it is done. I first began performing at the University of Alabama in the late 1970's when I was encouraged by friends to perform at the local coffeehouse. It was a very unnatural experience for me. I wanted to face my fears and as an elective the next semester signed up for a speech class. I had no idea of what to talk about during our weekly speeches and eventually extracted all my favorite jokes from the late night show with Johnny Carson who often hosted comedians. I would then take this material and fabricate absurd stories for the speech class. After torturing my classmates I would then venture over to the local weekly coffeehouse and unleash my best on the audience.

I also observed my friends and other performers at the coffeehouse and took note of what did or didn't work (most of it didn't!). I was drawn towards things to do and things NOT to do. Among the Do's included developing original material, effective spontaneity, graciousness to the crowd, sincerity, good pacing and momentum, quality sound, diversity of music, elements of surprise, solid technique and musicianship and the use of restraint. I emulated the musicians who allowed themselves to become immersed in their playing.

The Don'ts included stage fright, constantly looking to the crowd for approval, poorly timed humor or simply tasteless material, playing out of tune, bad rhythm, poor sound, lack of confidence, self-importance, trying too hard, or simply playing too long.

Following my college years I began to take notes on my experiences and traveling adventures. The comments from other people might have gone unnoticed if I had not logged them in some fashion. At least at this point of my career I was creating my own material and it was based on actual events, dialogue or situations. I believe that this is when I actually started to develop both the spoken and musical material to allow a performance to become more palatable for an audience.

Always try to keep in mind that you never know who will be in the audience. I played for the people who DID show up, not the ones who DIDN'T. In other words, whether there is an audience of 4 people or 4,000, I have always tried to put on a good show not only for them but also for myself. I have often used the analogy that a good film doesn't care who is in the audience. It can be the film's world premiere or playing on a Tuesday night in a small town for six people in a theater. It's still the same movie. Be the movie. And be a good one. You will never regret your effort, and certainly neither will your audience.

I also attempt to warm up a little bit before a performance. Sometimes I think of it as a sport, as even professional athletes warm up before they go play. To perform at an effective level, it never hurts to run through a few chords, patterns, scales or simply take a deep breath and relax.

Over the years I have had the privilege to share the stage with many well-known musical acts including Vassar Clements, Warren Zevon, Richard Thompson, John Prine, John McEuen, and comedians Harry Anderson, Louie Anderson, and Richard Lewis. I have played festivals in blistering heat, freezing cold, indoors, outdoors, with great sound systems, terrible ones and in many other environments. Once you have played in a situation, whatever it is, you have that experience under your belt. The next time you find yourself in a similar situation, you will find that you have something in your past to draw from which will allow you to make the most of it and actually take advantage of the experience.

Chapter Fifteen: Studio Tips

The following is a reprint from the 1998 article that appeared in Disc Makers *fastFORWARD* Summer/Fall 1998 newsletter. Since writing this article, I now feel it necessary to offer some additional thoughts on the subject of recording.

• When preparing your budget, record the tunes planned for the CD at home (a cheap tape deck will suffice) and gauge, as accurately as possible, the amount of studio time involved.

• Practice many takes of each tune and listen back over at least a couple of months, disregarding the quality of the recording, for subtle details that either delight or bug you. Many times you're in for surprises.

• Play one of your selections in your own living room. When the tune is over ask yourself how your body feels. If you're not relaxed ask yourself why. Then try again. Keep this relaxed and confident frame of mind when in the studio (easier said than done!)

• Practice breathing exercises if you're having trouble relaxing, and take plenty of time to warm up before judging yourself too harshly. Consider not playing the entire tune from start to finish. Work on sections as if they were puzzle pieces and then bridge the segments.

• Focus on your timing. The best thing I ever did for my playing was to work constantly with a metronome keeping in mind both timing and the idea of not letting any tunes go stiff. The metronome can also tell you where certain tunes "live."

• Select a theme for your recording. What's the point? What are you trying to say about yourself with this work? Allow some tunes intended for the recording to dissolve if they're not working. Save them for next time or another theme.

• If you're recording, a solo guitar piece that is particularly difficult, for example, consider recording in fragments or phrases. Studios have excellent editing capabilities. Remember that this is NOT a live performance. You're making a record.

• Beware of too many opinions. Trust a few, consider the source, but in the long run you usually know best.

• Play with the sequence of the tunes. Not only is your first tune the most important, but probably the first three or four. You want to hook your critics and listeners.

• Don't over-listen to the recordings. Take breaks to avoid burnout. After some time, if you don't rush and you don't burnout you'll be able to hear and "feel" things more objectively.

• Don't let the recording go out the door until you're sure it's right. When you are though, live with it. It's a page in your diary.

Additional Studio Tips

In addition to these suggested studio tips here are some other considerations.

- Ask ahead of time about better rates for block booked periods.

- Ask about cancellation policies. There may be times when you need to ask a favor and must move a scheduled session, or your engineer may need a favor from you to fit something in according to his/her schedule. Neither of you should abuse this privilege and it should be the exception, not the rule. Frequent alterations can upset the focus of a project, which can be crucial to its success.

- Be clear from the start on whether or not the engineer intends to charge you for time related to equipment failure problems on your part or their part, how interruptions will be handled (such as phone calls, surprise visits, etc.). In other words, if you are requesting a closed session find out if they are either willing or able to accommodate your needs.

Photo Credit: Wayne Brown

- With all that being said, understand too that the environment of a recording studio can be as a friend of mine once said, a *real pressure cooker!* There is money on the line and time invested away from touring, friends and family. The music that is close to you is also under a microscope and you must be aware that you are on the engineers turf and they can understandably become as sensitive about you telling them how to do their job as you are of them commenting on your work. Ideally, both parties should project an air of fun,relaxation,respect, professionalism, dedication and teamwork. Be aware too that towards the end of the project there will be a sense of urgency to *just get it out*. Do not be tempted. The finishing touches are far more than just the icing on the cake. That extra attention to detail is essentially the defining moment of the project.

Chapter Sixteen: Touring Tips and Road Stories

My band just released a CD and we want to set up a tour. Can you give us some tips on touring?

One of the best pieces of advice I can give concerning touring would be to take care of yourself. You need to constantly address both your physical *and* mental health.

I generally try to keep in mind the basics. Eat right, sleep right, and get some amount of exercise (and I don't mean just carrying your guitars up a flight of stairs to a gig!). On the front end of a tour I usually try to find a grocery store and stock up on non-perishable items which I can always have on hand in an emergency, such as apples, bananas, nuts, granola bars, juices, water, etc. For you it might be kidney beans and moose lips. To each his own.

Having a *detailed* map handy is always crucial as well. Hotel road guides and a plan to suit your style never hurt. I like to travel for a couple of hours at night after a show if it is not too late. The roads seem to be less traveled at that time and I am usually a little bit wound up after playing anyway and can get some of the drive out of the way. However, be forewarned that you should have a hotel destination in mind and secured with a credit card or you may be sleeping in your car! In other words, planning is of the essence. Although I have to admit that for my style I like to be as spontaneous as possible, since I hate getting locked into a situation if I decide to be *on the move* at the last minute. Be aware too of weather and road conditions and special events in certain towns. If you are not careful, you may find yourself in a real pickle if you are trying to find a hotel during the annual NASCAR event.

Photo Credit: Gill Winter, Flying Piglets, New Zealand.

It is also advisable to have various methods of contact such as destination phone numbers of people who are expecting you, a cell phone, someone you can call in an emergency, AAA or a road carrier service, extra strings, patch cords, batteries, cash and a credit card if possible for emergencies. Pace yourself physically and mentally. Don't overdo it and keep in touch with family and friends; this helps with occasional loneliness and isolation, and maintains your sanity if you are in it for the long haul.

Lastly, try to have fun. I tend to be somewhat of a tourist and as I go from town to town I try to take in the flavor of new regions, landmarks, historical locations and people.

Can you tell us some of the most interesting or bizarre things that have happened to you while touring on the road?

Photo Credit: Richard Gilewitz

Sometimes it's not just what happened, it's what some people say. In one case it involved a first grader. I had been asked at the end of a concert one evening if I would be willing to play for a classroom of first graders the following day. I obliged thinking, "This'll be easy". Don't ever think that!! Before I had arrived at the school, a friend of the teacher's decided to invite her class over and eventually the principal of the school became involved and she invited the entire school (nobody ever asked me!). They moved the event outdoors behind the school and after playing a couple of tunes I looked down into the *mosh pit* of first graders clustered up against the stage and asked if there were any questions. One of the kids stood up, raised his hand and asked, "Are most of the people who like the music you play dead?" I immediately signed up to play twenty more schools that year.

During one of my many sponsored guitar seminars a particular event was held (I won't mention the state) in New Jersey where the music store sold guitars and wigs. If that wasn't odd enough, on the way out at the end of the night I did a double take and noticed a fish bowl sitting on the counter. The sign on the bowl simply read, "earplugs - 3 for $1".

On another occasion I was billed as an opening act for David Bromberg and the venue was outdoors with a large sandpit in front of the stage. The soundman had all the sound equipment set up approximately 100 feet in front of the stage. During my sound check I noticed the soundman was taping down all the cords extending from the stage in the dirt with duct tape. Before long another Einstein waltzed along and tripped on his masterpiece and, of course, all the cords came up in the air since obviously tape doesn't stick to dirt. Instead of realizing this, the soundman went back to his van to find more duct tape and started over.

I was once double-booked with a rap artist. We decided to alternate songs. (I remember a huge guy standing in the middle of the dance floor grinning from ear to ear, shaking his head from side to side...he came up to me after my 2nd tune, smiled, and said, "I'm gonna help you get outta here!").

Chapter Seventeen: Alternate Tunings

While in alternate tunings, do you locate all the chords?

When I am in alternate tunings, I usually do not "re-find" all the chords. I generally search for pairs of strings, bar chords, and additions to bar chords while experimenting with variations around the pairs. Capturing moods or melodies and avoiding predictability are also a plus. If the tune can't stand alone, I throw it away. "Echoing Gilewitz" is a good example of a tune that did work out well with two left-hand fingerings and the 3rd and 4th pair of strings containing a melody.

What are your thoughts on tunings?

Take your time. Be sure your instrument is tuned accurately. There is nothing like a poorly tuned instrument to absolutely kill the music.

Train your ear. If you choose to use a chromatic tuner, you may want to consider using it as a source for just one note. Then, tune by ear. Follow up with the tuner as a checking device. This allows for continued *ear training*.

Check your tuning periodically. Playing, string bending, temperature changes, etc. may all contribute to putting your instrument out of tune, especially after applying new strings.

Rely on harmonics, fretted notes, and interval relationships within chords (from string to string) when tuning your instrument. One good way to check the intonation of your instrument is to play the string's harmonic at the 12th fret, then play the *note* at the 12th fret. If what you are hearing is way off, you may want to have a luthier or repairman check your instrument's intonation. A neck or saddle adjustment may be required.

What tunings do you mainly use?

Drop *D* Tuning (6 to 1 or low to high) - (D A D G B E)
When changing from standard to drop-*D* tuning, lower the sixth string down one whole step. Match pitches with the fourth string played open. They should be one octave apart. Compare also the pitches at the seventh fret on the sixth string with the fifth string played open. These should sound in unison with one another.

Open *G* Tuning (D G D G B D)
When tuning from standard to open *G*, lower the sixth, fifth, and first strings down one whole step. Compare pitches between the sixth and fourth strings played open, the fifth and third strings played open, and the fourth and first strings played open. Each of these pairs should be one octave apart. The seventh fret on the fifth string should be in unison with the open fourth string. The fifth fret on the sixth string should be in unison with the open fifth string. (Remember, your fifth string is now tuned to a *G*.) Finally, the third fret on the second string should be in unison with first string played open.

Note: for open *Gm* tuning **(D G D G B♭ D)**: same as open *G* except you must lower your second string one half step from *B* to *B♭*. The fourth fret on the second string should be in unison with the first string played open.

Open *D* Tuning (D A D F♯ A D)
When tuning from standard to open D, drop the sixth, second and first strings down one whole step. Drop the third string down one half step. Compare pitches between the open sixth and fourth strings, the fourth and the first strings played open, and the fifth and second strings played open. Each of these pairs should be one octave apart. The seventh fret on the sixth string should be in unison with the fifth string played open. The fifth fret on the second string should be in unison with the first string played open. The fourth fret on the fourth string should be in unison with the third string played open. The third fret on the third string should be in unison with the second string played open.

Note: For open *D modal* tuning **(or D A D G A D)**: same as open D, except the third string remains a G.

Open *C* Tuning (C G C G C E)
When tuning from standard to open *C*, drop the sixth string two whole steps, drop the fifth and fourth strings one whole step, and raise the second string by one half step. Compare pitches between the fourth and second strings played open, the fifth and third strings played open, and the sixth and fourth strings played open. Each of these pairs should be one octave apart. The fourth fret on the second string should be in unison with first string played open. The fifth fret on the third string should be in unison with the second string played open. The seventh fret on the fourth string should be in unison with the third string played open. The seventh fret on the fifth string should be in unison with the fourth string played open. The seventh fret on the sixth string should be in unison with the fifth string played open.

Master Tuning Diagram

String	Standard	Drop 'D'	Open 'G'	Open 'D'	Open 'C'
①	E	E	**D** (-1)	**D** (-1)	E
②	B	B	B	**A** (-1)	**C** (+1/2)
③	G	G	G	**F♯** (-1/2)	G
④	D	D	D	D	**C** (-1)
⑤	A	A	**G** (-1)	A	**G** (-1)
⑥	E	**D** (-1)	**D** (-1)	**D** (-1)	**C** (-2)

Boldface strings indicate that the pitch is altered from standard tuning. For example, **D** (-1) indicates that the string is to be tuned to a D, one whole step below the normal pitch of the string.

Also, remember the number ① in the string column of the diagram indicates the **high** string (the string closest to the floor) and the number ⑥ indicates the **low** bass string (the string closest to your nose!).

Chapter Eighteen: Fingernails and Fingerpicks

How do you take care of your fingernails and do you use fingerpicks?

Fingernail care for guitarists is a real interesting subject. I have heard stories of some individuals using super glue and tissue paper, acrylic treatments, and even ping-pong ball parts to create nails! (I actually went the super glue route myself, although at one point I considered using a flake cereal such as *Wheaties* and a drop of milk since they adhere so well to the bowl when not finished.)

I also realize some people prefer to use metal fingerpicks and plastic thumbpicks. I used to go this route, although over time I have come to feel that much better tone and control can be had by just using the bare fingers and fingernails. So I eventually shed my *Freddy Krueger Starter Set* and currently use very short nails on my right hand, which I file with the finishing side of a nail file followed by 400 sandpaper to smooth out the edges.

Another consideration, if you choose the fingernail approach, is to train yourself to reach for things with your left hand (or right hand for you lefty's picking with the left hand!) and slow down! Many times my nails have broken when I was rushing and reaching with my right hand for a door handle during cold weather or simply not paying attention. People have asked what I do if I break a nail. I don't do anything. Audiences (and I) just won't hear those notes until it grows back!

Chapter Nineteen: Speed Playing

How do you develop speed?

A great deal of speed comes with efficiency, timing, balance and economy of motion. Also, you must develop a willingness to practice slowly and *program* the motor functions into your right hand. Using the proper fingers without tripping over themselves is crucial. In other words, a great deal of your playing should come from a *borrowing* technique so that the same right-hand finger is NOT used twice in a row.

Breath control, relaxation, utilization of a metronome, and a great number of repetitions all play a role. Also, the focus and practice of difficult passages as well as segues from bar to bar, phrase to phrase are extremely important. This all helps to build confidence with the tune and after a time, the piece should almost seem to cruise along on its own. At this point you *ride* the piece instead of the piece *riding* you!

Chapter Twenty: Don't You Run Out of Breath and Get Tense?

Do you ever tense up when you play and catch yourself holding your breath?

Yes, or at least I used to find myself holding my breath during difficult tunes or when I felt I was losing the audience. I would also notice other parts of my body tensing, such as the shoulders, jaw, lips,… oh, and the brain. I don't seem to stiffen up while playing as much anymore, since it was a problem I eventually addressed.

In order to train myself to relax while playing, I would consciously focus on taking a breath during certain passages of a tune. Trust me, the air will go out of you by itself! By isolating and letting go of each tension point, the body begins to relax. Sometimes just letting go of ego and insecurity can relieve all the tension simultaneously. You can almost feel yourself *unlock* when you don't take it all so seriously.

By learning how to relax while playing, my posture has improved, my rhythm stays in the pocket, and I do not get as tired during a concert. It has become second nature to me to catch myself tensing up. If my timing becomes rushed or my neck becomes stiff, I know that I must take deep breaths and relax.

In addition, when I'm relaxed my audiences seem to sense that I am enjoying myself. This gives them the permission they needed to sit back and enjoy the concert.

One time I was so relaxed while playing that, after completing a tune, I noticed the applause coming from behind me. Opening my eyes I saw that I had completely turned around on my swivel stool to face the back of the stage.

Chapter Twenty One: Right-Hand Attack and Position

Can you tell us about your right-hand position and attack?

I use two hand positions depending on the tune and the effect I want from my playing. Generally, I tend to use a hand position that allows for the fingers to pick almost straight up toward the ceiling (perpendicular to the strings) with the right thumb extended out to the left of the hand when looking down. The thumb is then nearly parallel with the strings. This position lends itself to a more percussive sound.

For a brighter attack (the non-percussive approach), I'll angle the thumb up slightly, causing a bow of the wrist in an outward position. Either of these positions will produce a slight bend or *angle* in the wrist. As a beginner or as an experienced player making this adjustment, in order not to hurt yourself, I advise you to be both careful and patient.

I have provided many special dynamic notations, along with both left and right-hand fingerings throughout the pieces in specific places, especially when finger selections may be in question. A great deal of your playing should come from a *borrowing* technique so that the same right-hand finger is NOT used twice in a row. This technique creates a right-hand balance that allows the fingers to avoid *tripping* over each other. (Much like jogging and using the same leg twice in a row!)

I generally use my thumb *(p)* for the bass strings 6, 5, and 4. The index *(i)*, middle *(m)*, and ring *(a)* are usually based out of the following three positions:

Position 1 (i,m,a - strings ③, ②, ①)
Position 2 (i,m,a - strings ④, ③, ②)
Position 3 (i,m,a - strings ⑤, ④, ③)

When plucking strings with your ring (a) finger, be sure to allow your little finger (pinkie) to move with it or *shadow* the ring finger so the two fingers move as a unit.

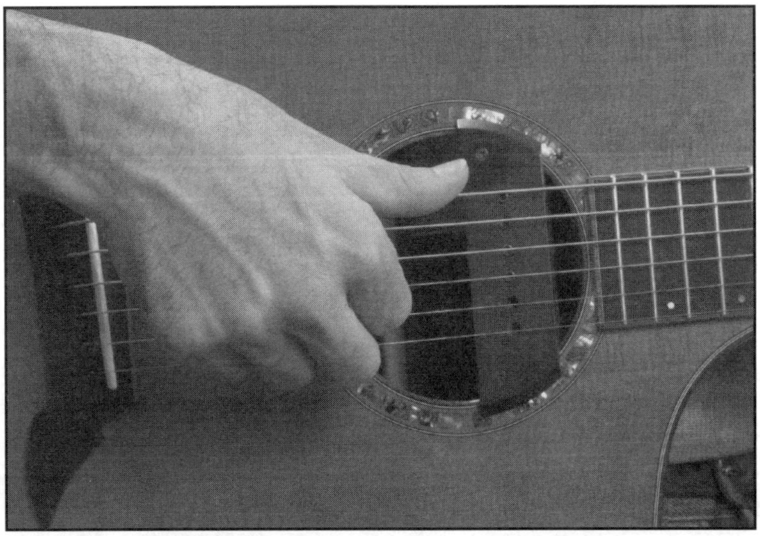

Photo Credits: Wayne Brown

Chapter Twenty Two: Words of Encouragement

What encouraging words can you share?

As I repeatedly stress to students in my private classes, and to attendees of the many guitar seminars I conduct: **THERE ARE NO REAL SHORTCUTS**. To become a truly accomplished player, it takes several years of dedication, practice, and a genuine affection for both the guitar and the music you choose to play. Whole proper technique, the use of a metronome, and good teachers make a great foundation, the player must also tap into the extraordinary library of material available. Play, practice and have fun. If you are not having fun, you won't do it. You should expect peaks and valleys but constantly look for ways to rekindle that interest - whether it's listening to another musician or another style of music, finding a different teacher, or indulging yourself with a new piece of music.

I strongly recommend that you collect both written and recorded music as well as instructional videos, attend music schools, workshops, and seminars. Study with teachers, play and practice privately, and involve yourself with musical social events whether it is an open mike night, coffeehouse, or house party. Music should be as much a social event as it can be a private one. There are great lessons to be learned from both environments.

Avoid excuses, criticism, blame, and gauging your natural talents, or supposed lack thereof. Through hard work and long-term dedication your efforts are almost guaranteed to pay off. Become your own *realistic* critic.

I recall a time when I played a legendary honky-tonk club named The Flora-Bama (located directly on the Florida/ Alabama line in Perdido Key, Florida). Another legend showed up to hear me play; Kenny Stabler, the former NFL quarterback and member of The Hall of Fame. I was flattered when he came up and told me how much he enjoyed my playing, but what had more of an impact on me that night was the story I heard about Kenny's comment to *Sports Illustrated* about an event held at The Flora-Bama - the infamous *mullet toss* competition. Basically, for $10 you get to enter the competition and are handed a dead mullet. As the contestants stand on the beach behind the Flora-Bama, they see how far they can throw the mullet. The winner gets a t-shirt. My understanding was that Kenny had won this competition every year, except for one when he claimed his mullet *slipped*. When *Sports Illustrated* arrived to witness this event they interviewed Kenny afterwards and asked him what his secret was for winning every year. Instead of stating the obvious, which to me was "well, I am a Hall of Fame NFL quarterback", Kenny simply said, "well, I just grab it and chuck it". My sentiments exactly.

The guitar. Just grab it and *play* it.

Mr Ki Chon Choi, my martial arts mentor.

Chapter Twenty Three: Picking Pattern Study Notes

I generally select my patterns with the right hand from one of two *families* of picking patterns, either from the arpeggio family or the alternating bass banjo-style family. Basically I think of arpeggios as at least two fingers played following a thumb strike and often three fingers. With the alternating bass style I consider the idea as a sequence of thumb-finger-thumb-finger with the variations including what I call inside rolls, forward rolls, pairings of fingers, and pinch patterns, along with the use of left-hand hammer-ons and pull-offs

Arpeggio notes:

• Play as evenly as possible with a comfortable metronome range from slowest to fastest, increasing this range over time as with the tremolo study.

• Unlike the tremolo study, put more emphasis on accenting certain notes as you play to add depth to the arpeggio technique.

• Allow the music to ebb and flow.

Tremolo notes:

• Be sure to play the four note sequences as evenly as possible.

• When changing to the next chord be sure not to *clip* off the last note of the tremolo. Work on the transition carefully.

• Find a range on the metronome from slowest to fastest and increase the range on 'both' ends over a 'long' period of time.

• Accent the middle or 'm' finger since it has a tendency to be the weakest initially.

• Watch your breathing and attempt to breathe rhythmically at the start of each measure. Try to allow the music to *breathe out* like a sigh. Like the arpeggio, the tremolo should also ebb and flow.

Hand Chart

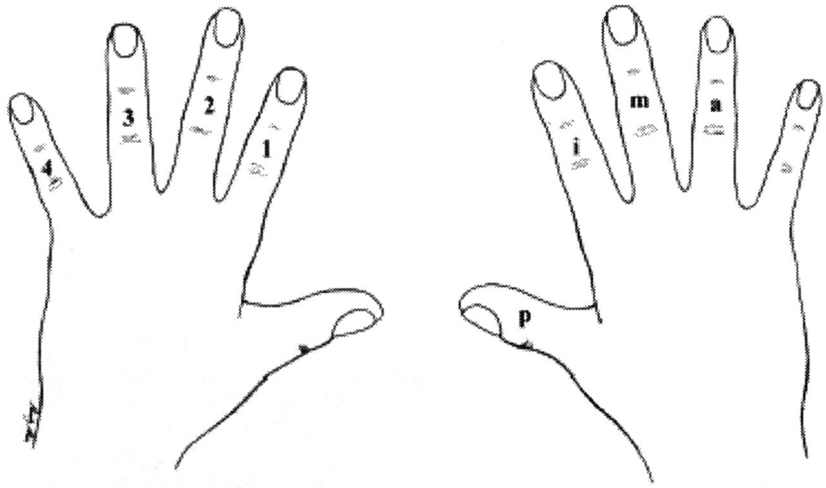

Left Hand **Right Hand**

Chapter Twenty Four: Historical Notes

"Echoing Wilderness"

I was inspired to write this tune in the late 70s at the University of Alabama. As one of my first serious endeavors at composing, the opening slide segment was my attempt to mimic a piece, "They Only Moved the Stage", by pedal steel player Cal Hand and guitarist Leo Kottke. Originally titled "The Vision", this opening section was also written as the result of an adventure in the woods at dusk when I almost *crawled* off a cliff while on my hands and knees searching for the trail.

The middle portion came from a friend of mine who did not play any instrument at all! He insisted, however, on directing me in playing a 12-string guitar with such comments as "Do something up high", "Now try those harmonic things again.", "Do a low thing somewhere twice."

The European group SKY, featuring classical guitarist John Williams influenced me in writing the final section. The piece in particular was "Watching the Aeroplanes", which generates a continuous swirling effect. With the ending still unwritten, I found myself searching for a closure after returning home from a day at Disney World in Orlando, Florida. The theme song from the "Main Street Electrical Parade" continually played in my head as I listened to the movie, *The Hunchback of Notre Dame* on television in the background. Just when the Hunchback realized that the beautiful damsel did not see him as Mr. Right, he vented his frustrations by dangling from the tower bells. The forces of SKY, Disney World, and the *Hunchback* collided in my head and the whole tune popped out perfectly.

On *A Shout Toward Noon* (Private Music), Leo Kottke recorded this final section of "Echoing Wilderness". Renamed by Kottke as "Echoing Gilewitz", this portion of "Echoing Wilderness" is included in this book. At one time it was a well-known morning *wake up* song on the radio in Japan. The full original 8-minute piece containing "Echoing Gilewitz" can be heard on *Synapse Collapse*. This piece also appeared in the May/June 2002 issue of *Fingerstyle Guitar Magazine*, coincidentally featuring guitarist John Williams whose European band SKY actually inspired the piece.

"The Maison Blanche Exit Song"

I began writing this piece in early 1980. While two friends fell asleep in front of a fireplace, I found myself alone with my own conversation and guitar. Staring into the flames, I fell into a simple three-chord pattern, a forward roll, and an attempt to put a mood and melody in the middle of a tune; I conjured up the entire song in less than an hour. I eventually dedicated the title in celebration of getting kicked out of a French cuisine restaurant in Washington, D.C. for not wearing socks. The restaurant, I understand, has since closed. I continue to feel that socks are optional.

"Mrs. Firecracker's Place"

Following one of my performances at a wonderful little room called McDibbs (sad to say, no longer in existence), film director Michael Wadleigh approached me and requested a composition for a sequel to his award-winning movie, *Woodstock*. His intention at the time was to film it in Black Mountain, North Carolina with the working title, "The Village at the End of the Universe". So utterly flattered with the request and challenge of this assignment, I named the piece before I wrote a single note. On my drive back home to Florida, I noticed a billboard advertising *Mrs. Firecracker's Place*. My first thought, while recalling Arlo Guthrie's famed hit, was, "Wow! Who would want to go to *Alice's Restaurant* when you can go to *Mrs. Firecracker's Place*!" Unfortunately, the film never happened. The tune did.

Performance Notes for Mrs. Firecracker's Place

The following are some specific notes, or more accurately, *observances* you may want to consider not only for this particular piece or the rest of the music contained in this book, but also for any pieces of music you consider for your future repertoire regardless of the instrument's tuning or the style you choose to play.

Some of the patterns listed in the Picking Patterns section of this book, or at least fragments of these patterns, are briefly explained here as they pertain to "Mrs. Firecracker's Place", merely as a sample of how they have been used in a composition. You may want to either consider some of these ideas when composing your own music or simply try to recognize them in other pieces you study or perform.

In the first half of measure 10 in "Mrs. Firecracker's Place" you will notice an ascending arpeggio played against a pinch pattern.

In measure 12 you will notice both an ascending and descending arpeggio played against a double pinch pattern (two in a row) contained within an alternating bass with *p* (right thumb).

In measure 13 through 16 note the use of pairs played with *m* and *a* or the right-hand middle and ring fingers.

Throughout measures 1-16 you will notice the right hand thumb and index, or *p* and *i* being used in the fashion of a plectrum or 'flatpick' as the right hand shifts back and forth between positions three and two as mentioned in Chapter 21.

Measure 17 combines the use of an alternating bass with both pinch patterns and arpeggio fragments (with the last fragment being a three-note descending arpeggio).

Measure 35 consists of a forward roll followed by an inside roll.

Measure 36 consists of a double pinch pattern within an alternating bass followed by an inside roll.

Measure 40 contains a triplet in the melody played against an alternating bass.

Throughout measures 55-62 you will notice an alternating bass with the right hand in position two (strings 4, 3, and 2) while using pull-offs and hammer-ons as well as pairs with *m* and *a* on the right hand. Notice the double picking sound you get on the fourth string by utilizing the alternating bass while in position two (the right thumb and index create a type of *ticka-ticka* sound in the middle of the music).

Measure 83 simply utilizes two forward rolls in a row.

In measures 99-102 and 107-110 be sure to bring out the fourth string with the right hand index *i* during performance. This attack allows for more of a three dimensional sound to your music.

Best of luck, and as I have mentioned earlier, consider using some of these patterns in your own compositions and observe them in other pieces of music. But above all, have fun!

(Performance Notes Continued)

"Pre-dawn Mourning"

At some point in the early 1980s, I wrote this piece in DADGAD, a popular modern tuning. I sat down in a room and wrote the entire piece in about 45 minutes. Composed on the 12-string, I was intrigued by the effect of the right thumb when playing down on the 3rd and 4th strings. The octave notes created a nice swirl as high notes were sounding on the downbeats in an arpeggio fashion. "Pre-dawn Mourning" was actually recorded using a 6-string guitar, however; it is still a mystery to me that I elected not to stick with the 12- string guitar. The title was coined by a biology professor at the University of Alabama while riding in an elevator with me. He liked the idea of spelling morning 'mourning'. The mood fit, so I used it.

"Jamaicalina"

Family members are often a source of inspiration and "Jamaicalina" is an example of putting together a tune to reflect those sources. Around the late 1980s, Jane, my wife at the time, had an affection for the island of Jamaica based on her earlier visits there. Since she grew up in North Carolina, I invented the title "Jamaicalina" in an attempt to somehow fuse her two worlds - bringing together an *islandy* rhythmic feel of Jamaica with a *coastal* swing of the Carolinas.

"Bilingual Fantasy"

"Bilingual Fantasy" is a piece I wrote while attending the University of Alabama during the late 1970s. I actually wrote it to get rid of a girl. I always thought music was written to attract a partner. Cynthia and I had gone out for six months but after the first month we realized we were not right for each other. We were only freshmen and had not developed any breaking up tools. Being too polite we just molted for another five months and one day I said, "Hey Cynthia, if I write a tune for you will you go away?" She was ecstatic and her face lit up like the first day she met me. "Sure", she said. Due to her lack of hesitation I selected a minor key and got to work. When I completed the tune she said it wasn't long enough. Realizing she knew nothing about music and did not play any instruments, I simply waited two weeks and then played it for her twice in a row. She was finally satisfied. (I miss her every time I play it!)

"Dirt to Dust"

"Dirt to Dust" was a piece I began writing in the mid 1990s and spent about two years completing, although it underwent many changes in the general feel during each live performance. This is the only piece I have composed in a G minor tuning which practically defined the mood when I had barely started. I envisioned a cross between a Clint Eastwood western theme and *Dr. Zhivago,* making it seem as if I were stuck in a desert yet feeling very cold. The end of the piece, which slows down considerably, employs a right-hand two-finger tapping method to target specific notes and bring out the melody, hopefully evoking a contemplative yet serene mood (watch out for those cold *desert snakes*!)

Track # 1

Arpeggio Exercise

Adapted from a study by
Dionisio Aguado

TAB edition by Richard Gilewitz

Track #2

Tremolo Exercise

TAB edition by Richard Gilewitz

Track #3

Picking Patterns

(Play each measure twice)

by Richard Gilewitz

Inside Rolls

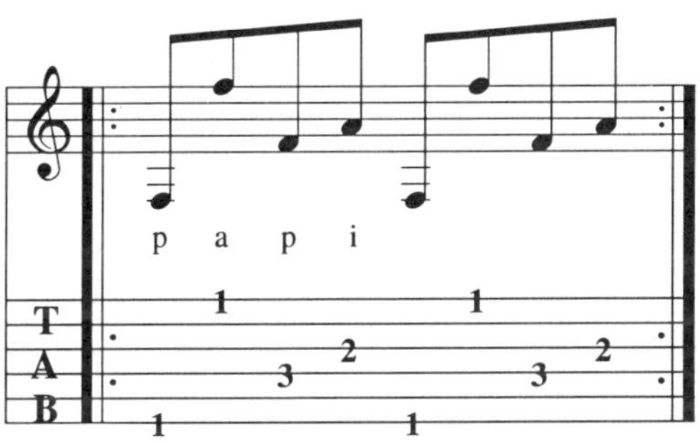

Track #4

Forward Rolls

Track #5

(Picking Patterns)

by Richard Gilewitz

Inside Rolls with Pairs

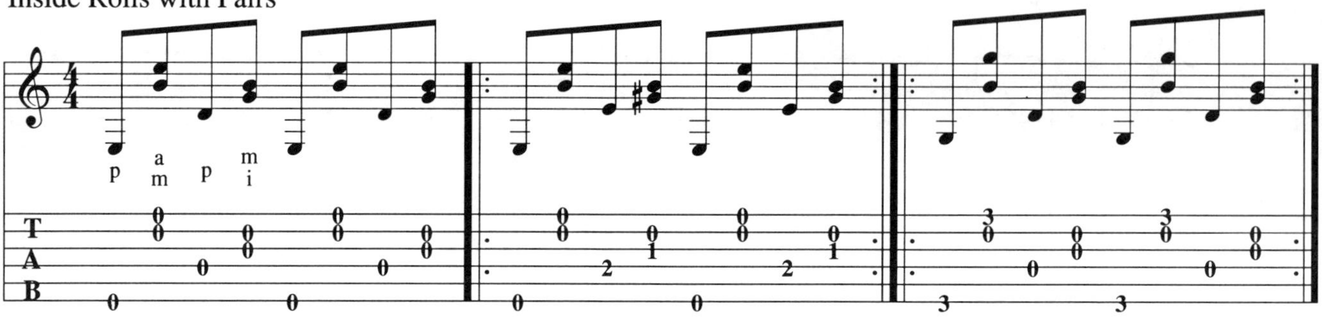

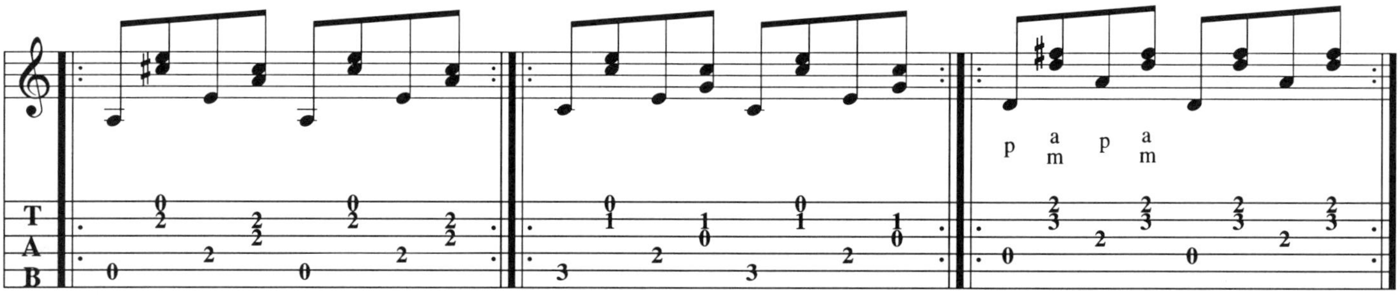

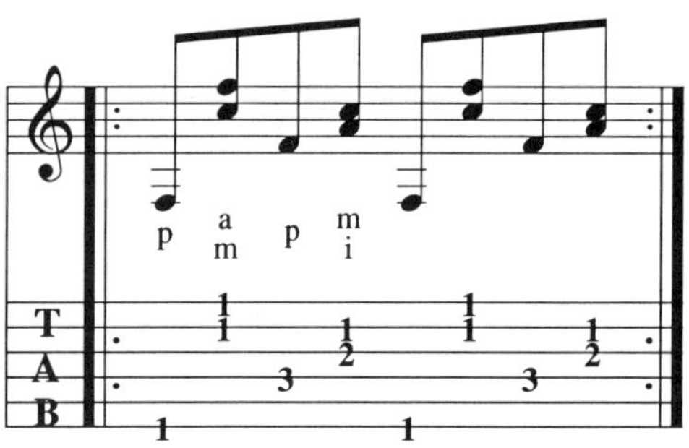

Track #6

Forward Roll with Pairs

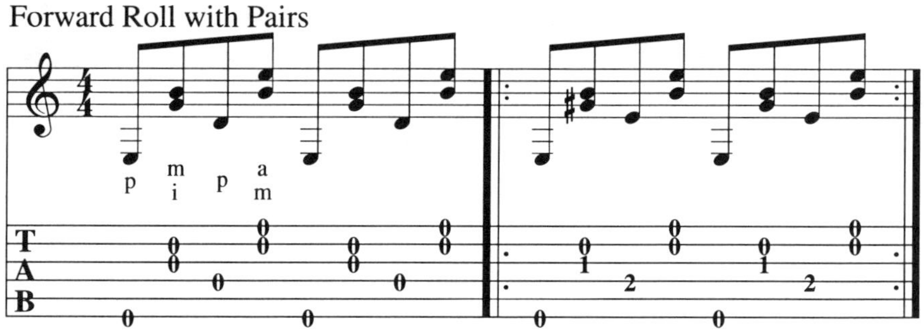

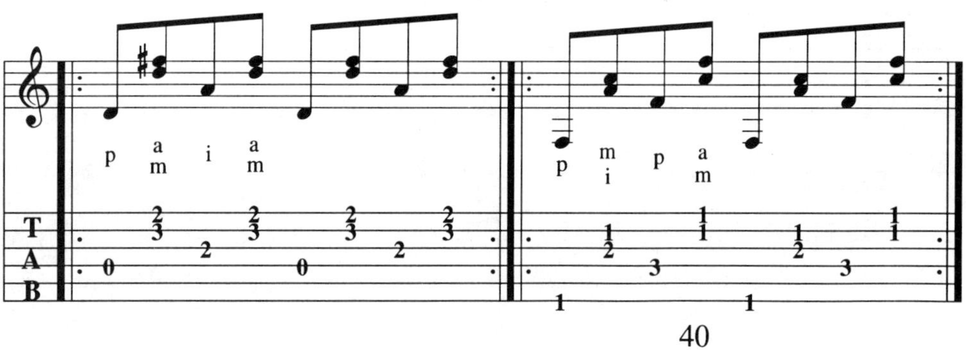

(Picking Patterns)

by Richard Gilewitz

Pinch Patterns

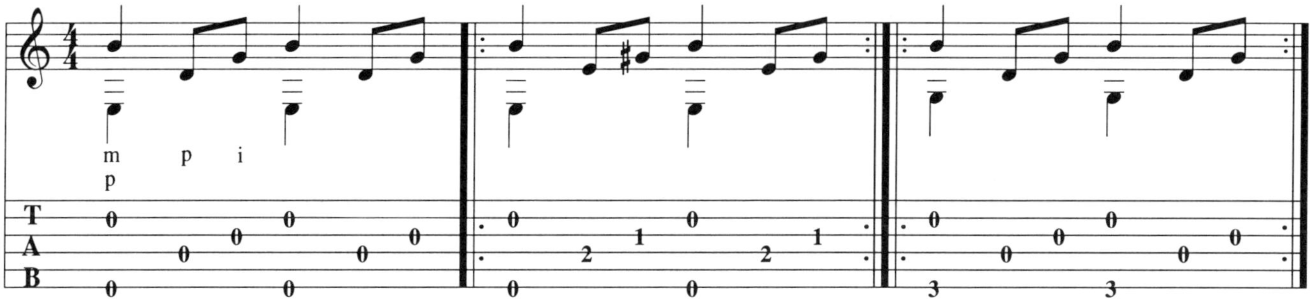

Track #8

Pinch Patterns with Pairs

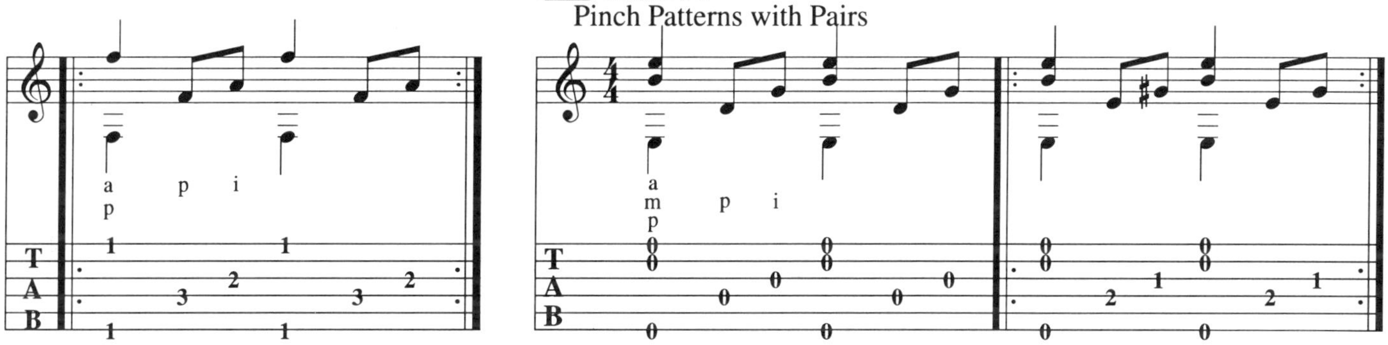

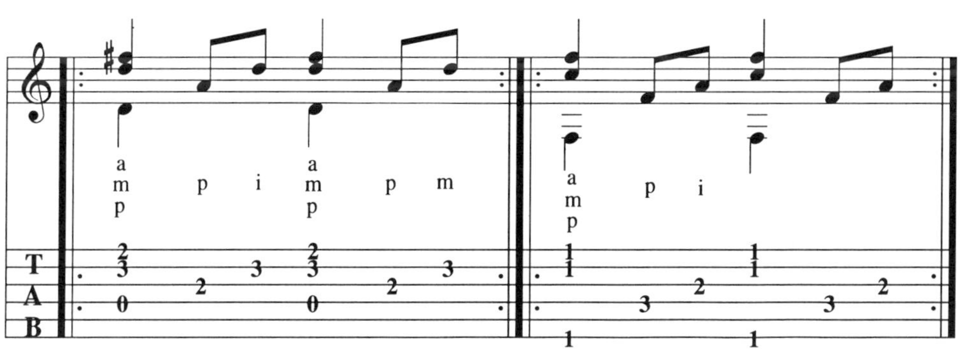

(note "i" substitution on "and" of beat 2)

(Picking Patterns)

by Richard Gilewitz

Arpeggio Patterns

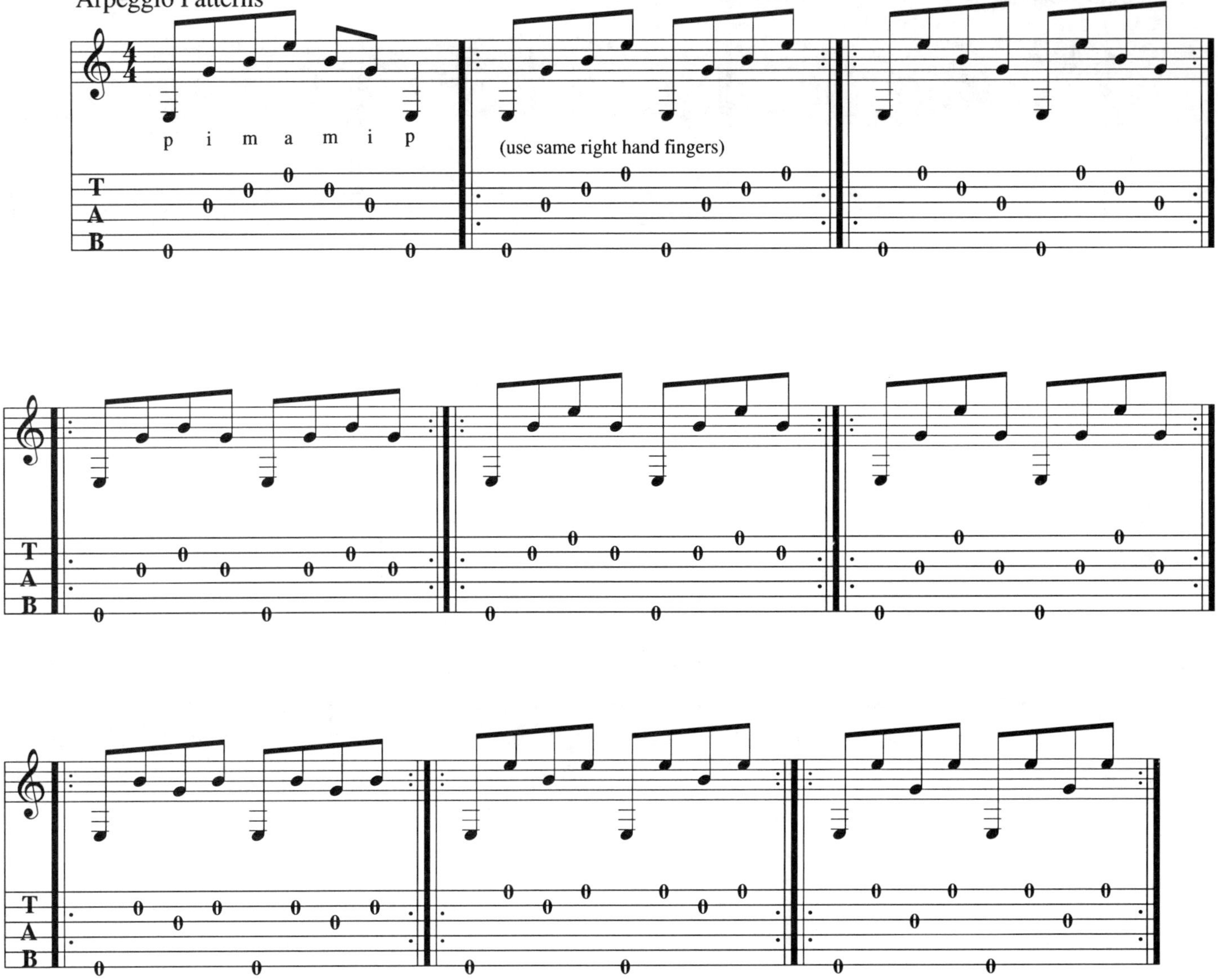

Extra Patterns

by Richard Gilewitz

Track #10

Hammer-Ons

Track #11

With Bass Movement

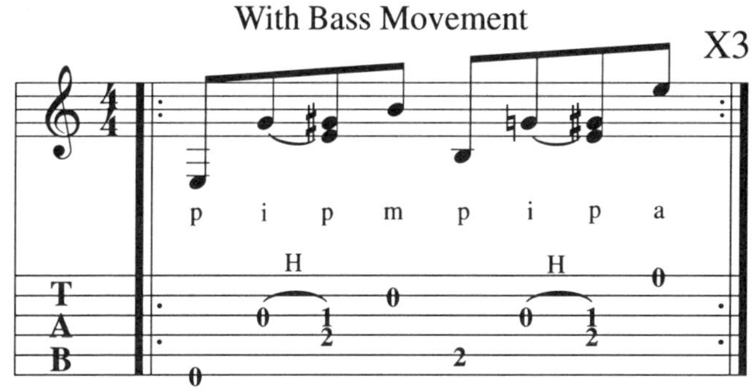

Track #12

With Pair

Track #13

Double Hammer-On

Track #14

Pull-Offs

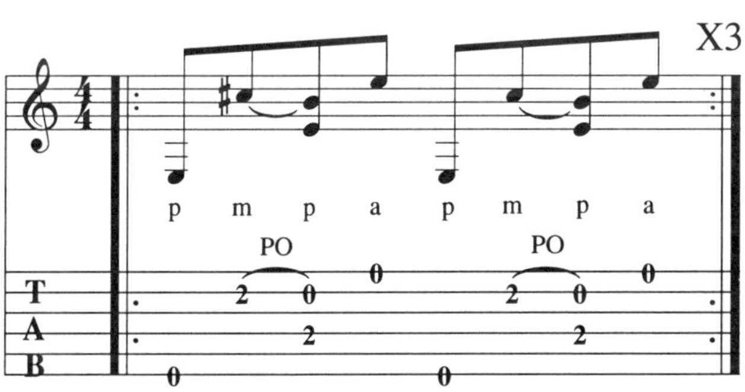

Track #15

With Bass Movement

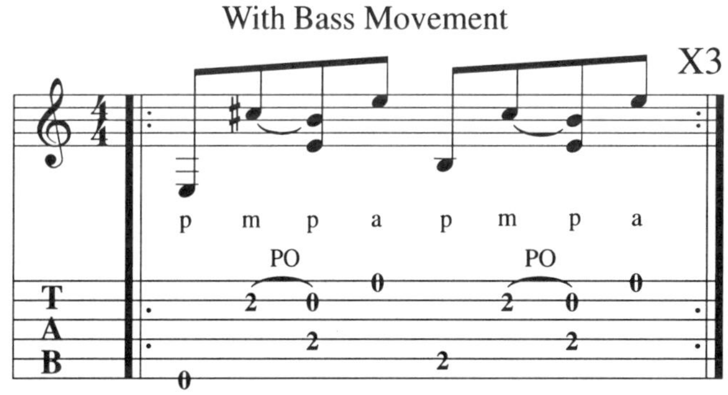

Track #16

With Pair

Track #17

Double Pull-Off

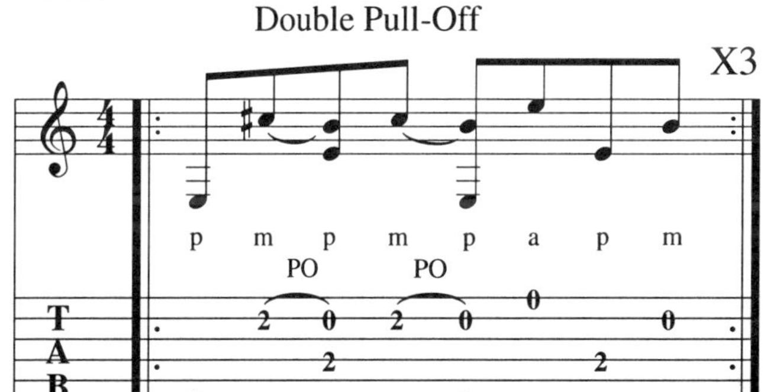

Echoing Gilewitz Patterns

Standard Tuning

by Richard Gilewitz

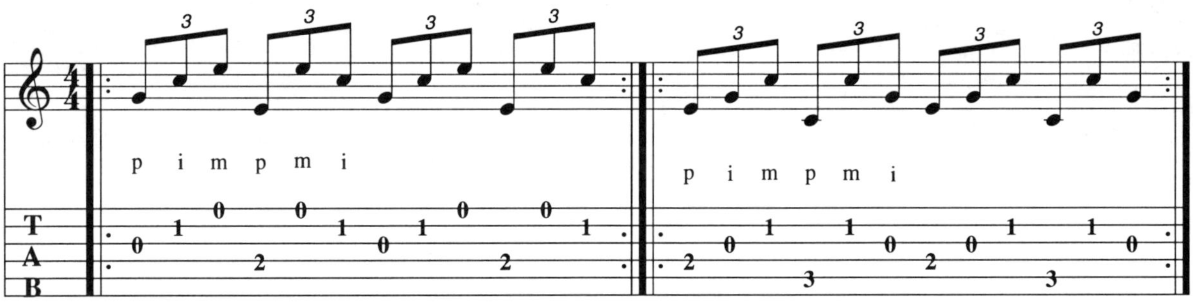

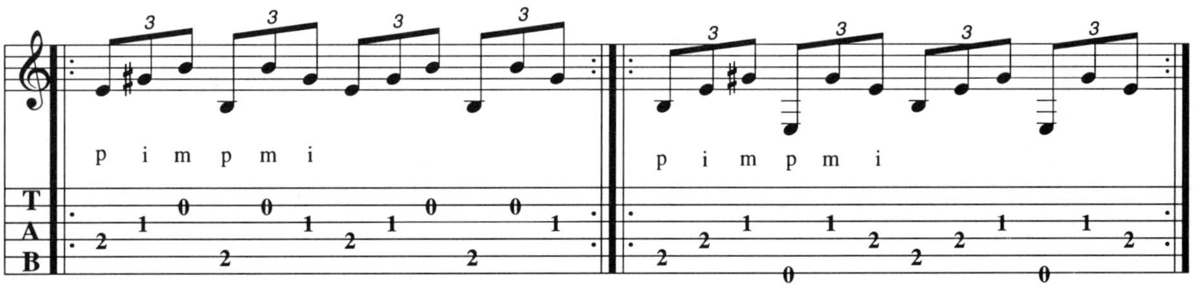

Track #19

Echoing Gilewitz

(excerpt from "Echoing Wilderness")

Tuning: D A D F♯ A D

by Richard Gilewitz

SL

23
25
27
29
31
33
SL

36
SL
SL
38
SL
40
42
44
46

* bend and release 2nd string harmonic one whole tone behind nut

Photo Credit: Michael Stock

Track #20

Maison Blanche Patterns

Standard Tuning

by Richard Gilewitz

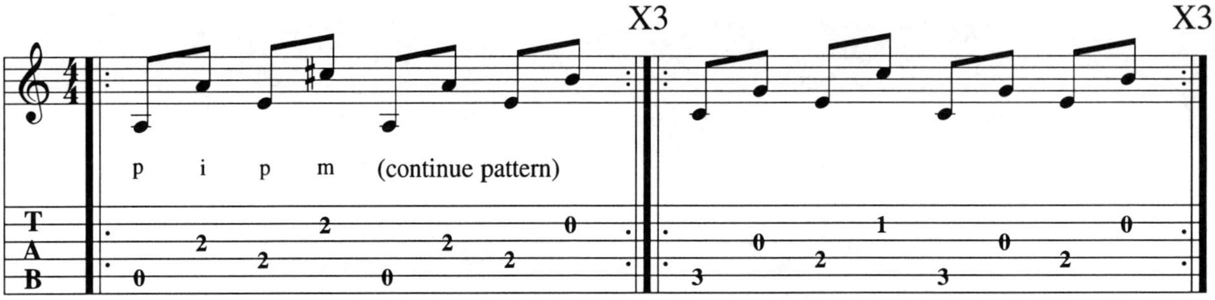

Track #21 The Maison Blanche Exit Song

Tuning: D A D G B E, Capo IV

by Richard Gilewitz

* measures 9 and 10 are played a total of 4 times (X3 indicates 3 repeats)

13
p i p i p i p m
SL H H
SL
16
SL H
SL
SL H
19
SL
SL
22
SL
p p i m i m i m a
p p
arpeggio roll
SL

SL
vibrato with fade
H
H
mute bass notes (including hammer-ons) with palm of right hand
H
H
PO
PO
PO
PO
H
H

SL
PO
arpeggio roll
p p i m i m i m a
p p
H
T
A
B

SL
arpeggio roll
SL
D.C. al Coda
SL
SL
Coda
rit.
off-set notes as in arpeggio

Track #22

Mrs. Firecracker's Patterns

Standard Tuning

by Richard Gilewitz

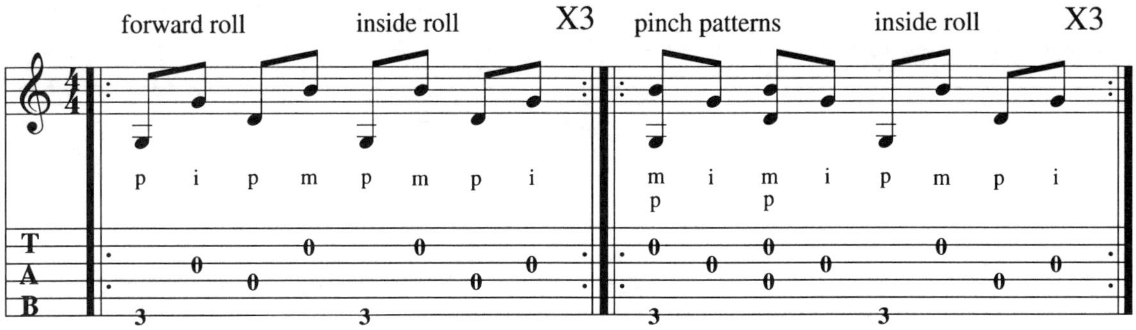

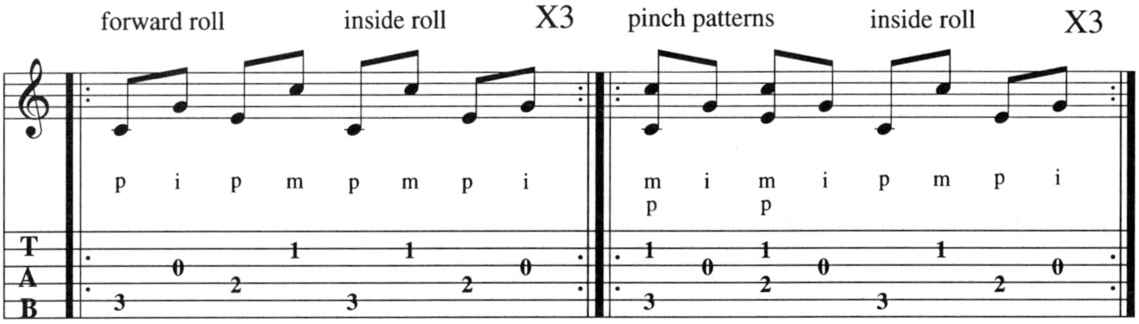

Track #23

Mrs. Firecracker's Place

by Richard Gilewitz

* Position alignment of right thumb to be parallel with strings and avoid collision with right index finger during upstrokes. All notes played with the left hand fingers are muted with a left hand quick releasefor measures 1-12, 27-30 and 117-124.

* measures 17 and 18 are played a total of 4 times (X3 indicates 3 repeats)

28
31
-1½
-1½
34
P
sl
37
H
rasqueado
40
3
H P
P

X3

57
P H P P H P
59
P H P H P H P H
61
P H P P H P H
63
66
p i p i p a p i
m
T
A
B

69
H P
72
sl
P
75
p i a
H P
P
78
H
H
P
81
right hand palm mute

84
87
90
93
96

99
P P P H
102
P sl sl P
105
sl sl sl sl H H
108
P H P
111
H H P H

X3
114
P P P
p a m p i p a m p i m
H P
117
120
123

Track #24

Pre-Dawn Mourning

Tuning: D A D G A D

by Richard Gilewitz

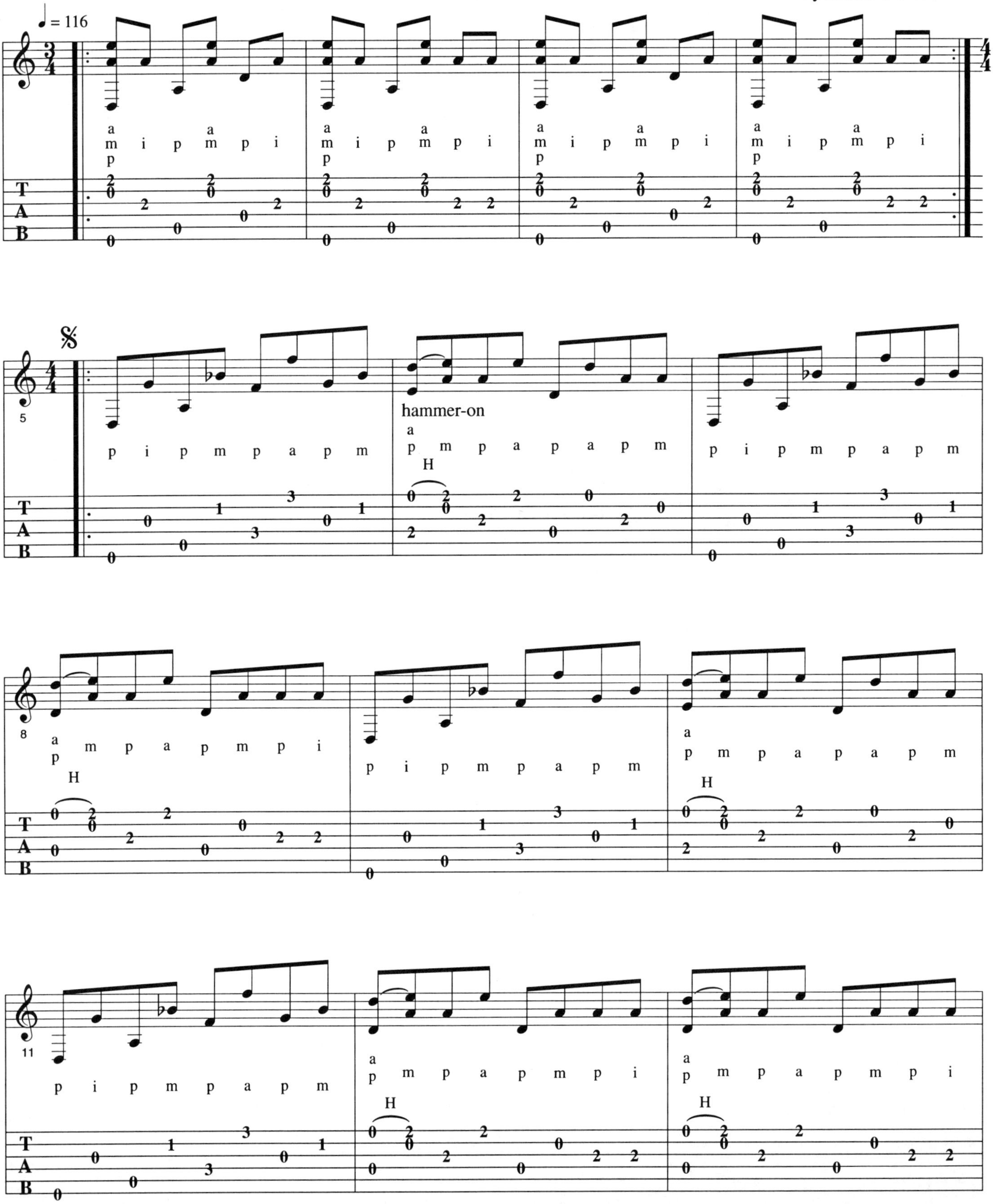

* measures 16 is played a total of 4 times
(X3 indicates 3 repeats)

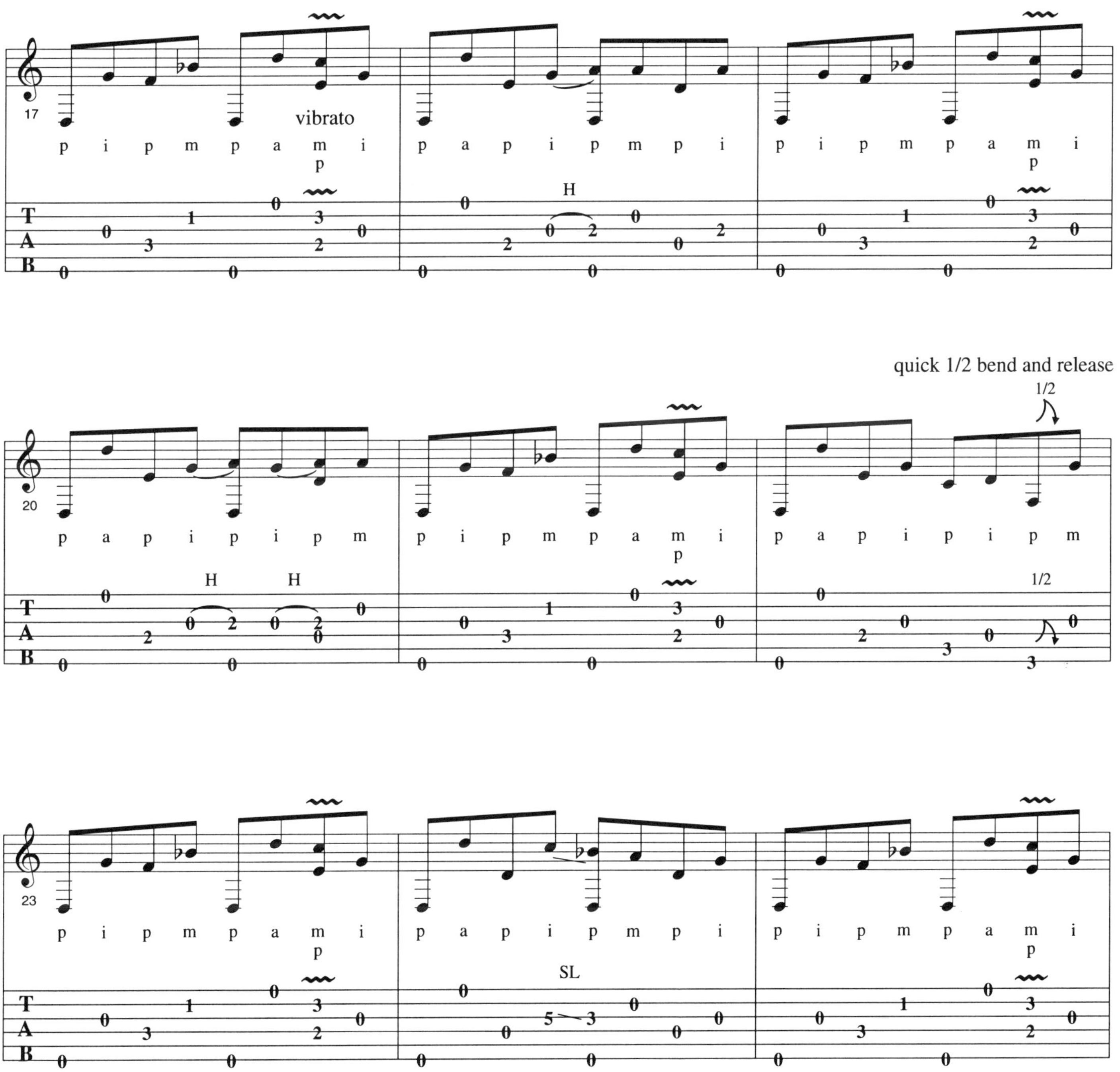

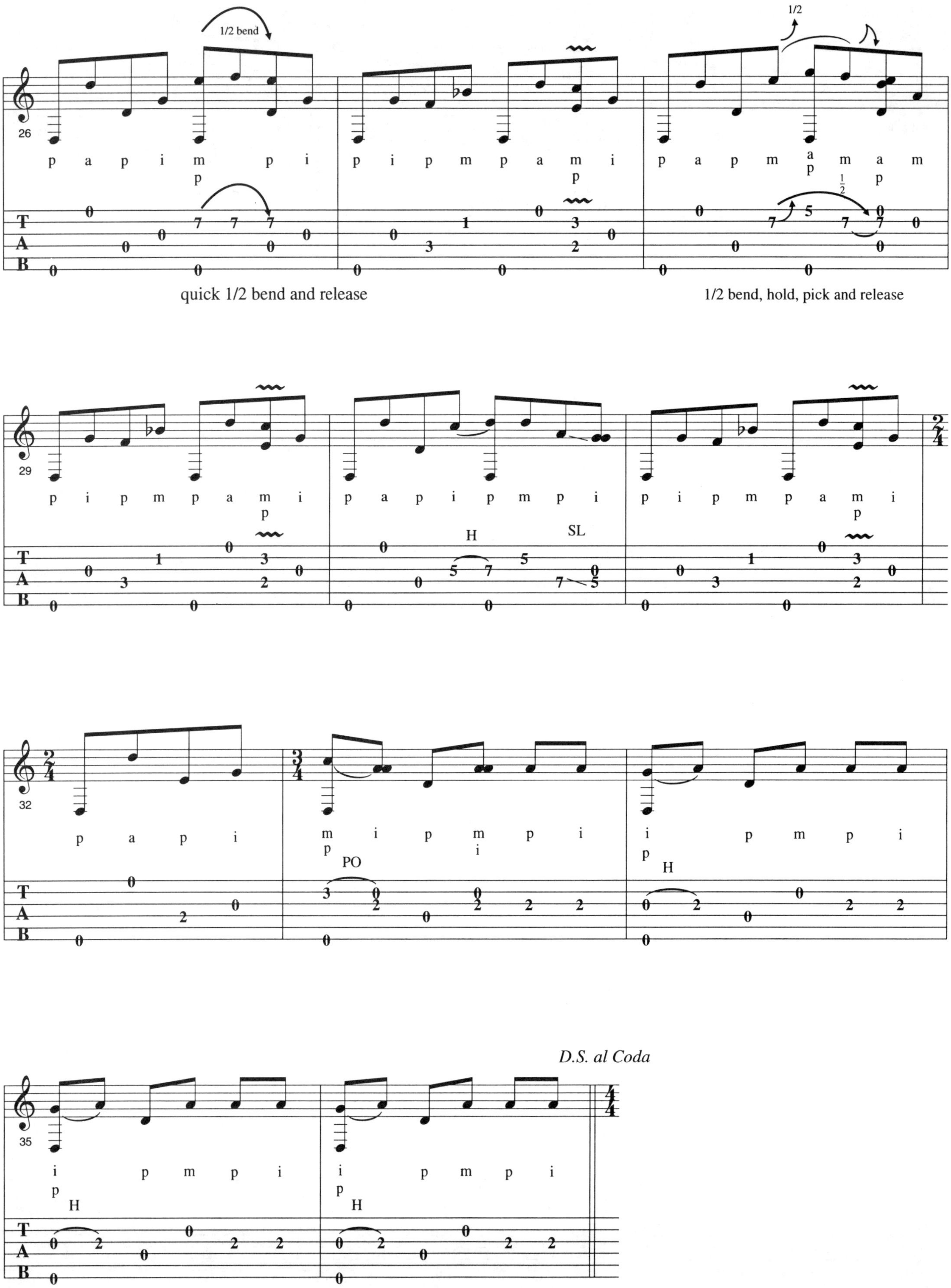
1/2 bend
1/2
quick 1/2 bend and release
1/2 bend, hold, pick and release
D.S. al Coda

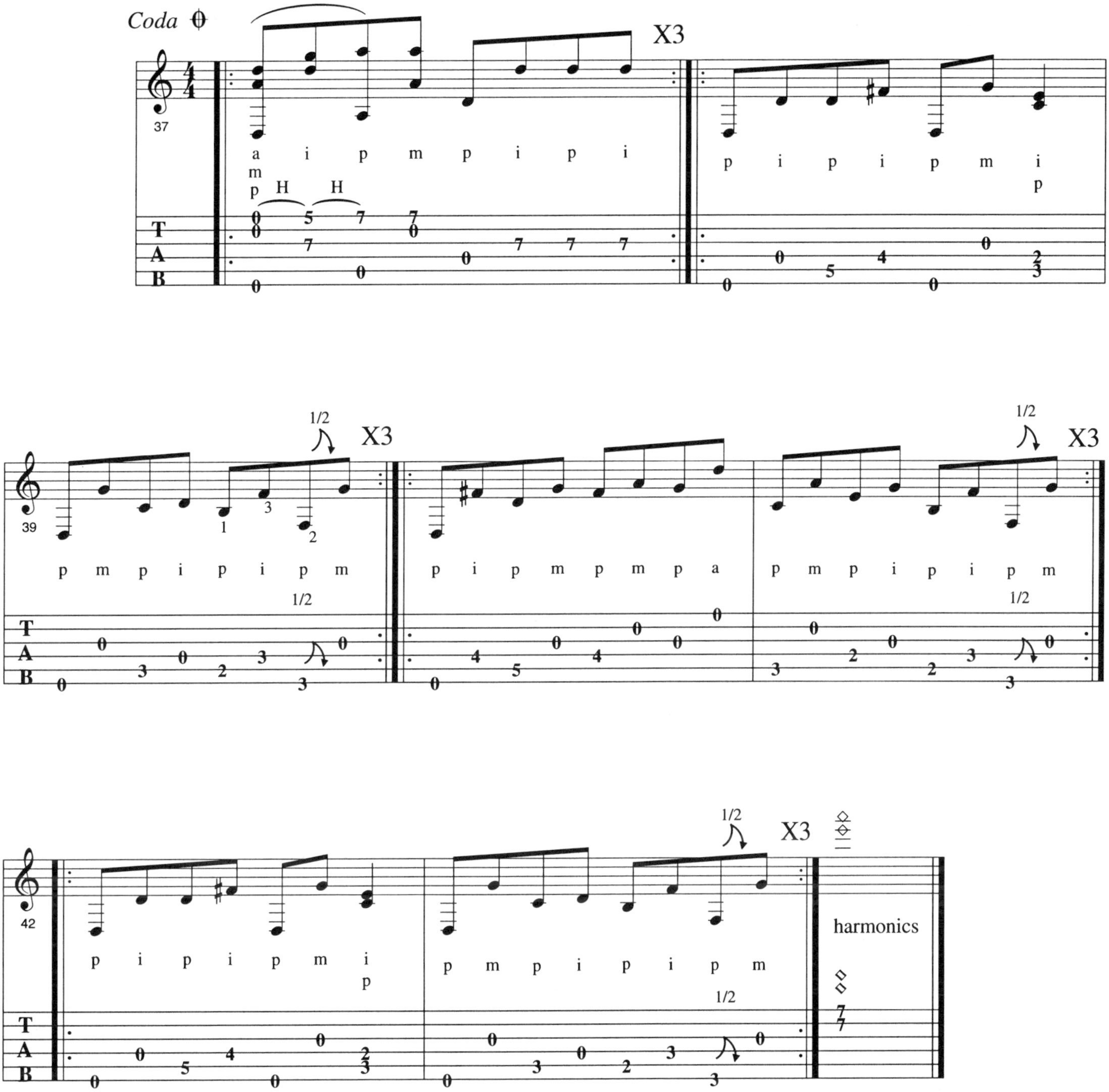
Coda
X3
X3
X3
X3
harmonics

Track #25

Jamaicalina

Tuning: C G C G C E

by Richard Gilewitz

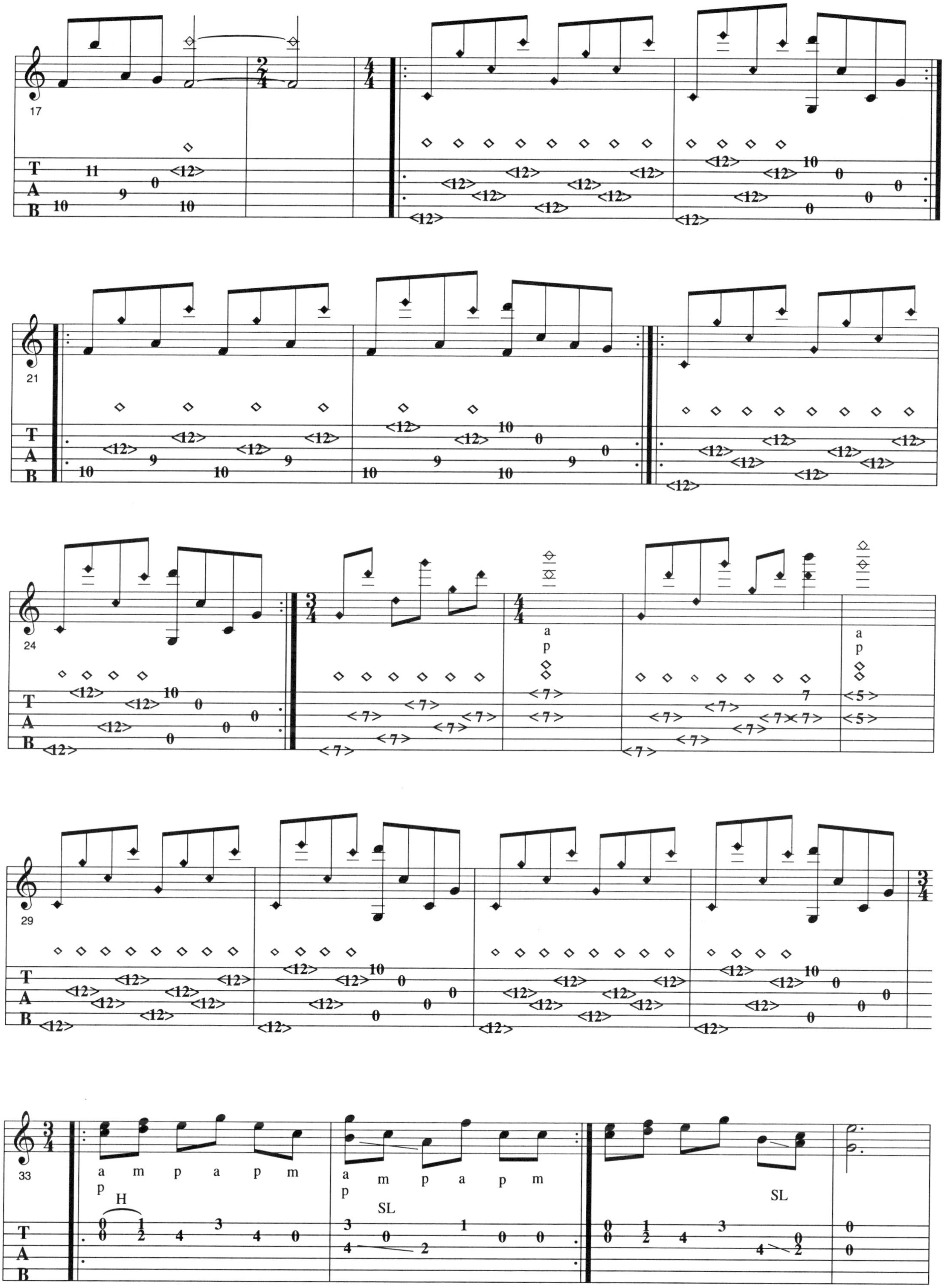
17
21
24
29
33
a p
H
SL
play measures 33 & 34, 3 times total

power strum with slides
H
SL
play measures 37 & 38, 3 times total
p m p a p m
grace note
PO
R

R
PO
SL
H
vibrato
X3
V

77
H
81
VII
p i p i
85
89
p i
93
p m

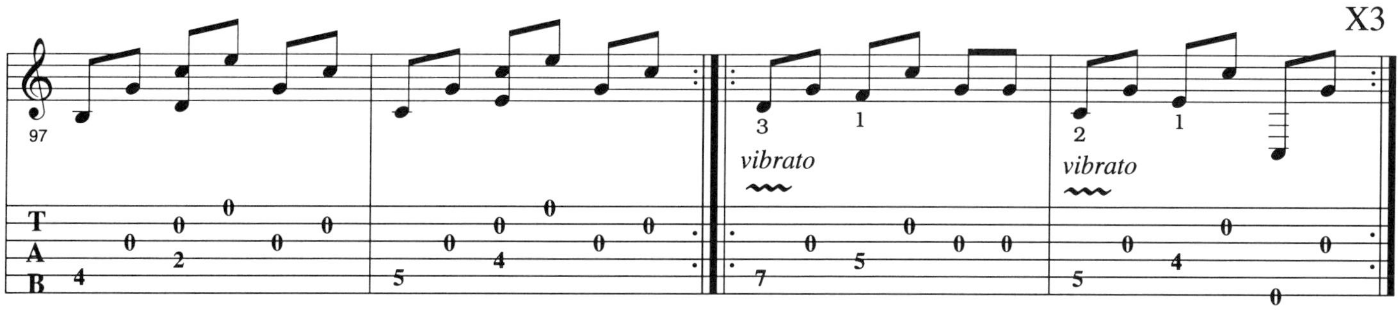

* measures 99-100 are played a total of 4 times
(X3 indicates 3 repeats)

117
H
121
H
125
129
vibrato
p i p i
133

fff
vibrato
muted strum
ff
p i p i
fff
muted strum
ff
vibrato throughout
p i p m p i
H
PO H PO H

"bounce" entire chord up and down for effect: measures 157-160

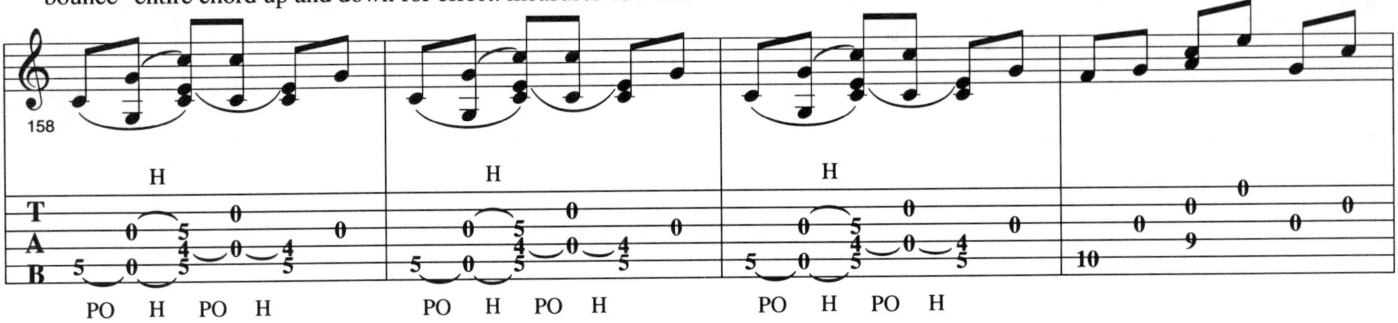

*measures 171 and 172 are played a total of 3 times
(X2 indicates 2 repeats)

178
H
182
p i p i
186
muted notes
190
rit.
SL
R
a m i p p
freely
195 arpeggio roll
p p p i m a

Track #26

Bilingual Fantasy

by Richard Gilewitz

Tuning: D A D G B E

15
p m p a p m
19
a
p m p m p i
power strum with thumb
23
27
31
vibrato

("p" strums strings ⑥, ④, ⑤ -
downstrum followed by "i, m, a")
*rasqueado-a m i

R R R R
SL
H
a m i p m a p m p i
rasqueado
R
SL

Track #27

Gypsy Minor (Intro to "Dirt to Dust")

Tuning: D G D G B♭ D

composed and transcribed by Richard Gilewitz

17
SL SL
SL
SL
SL SL
SL
m i m i
p p
21

Track #27

Dirt to Dust

Tuning: D G D G B♭ D

by Richard Gilewitz

mute
p i m i m i m a
p p p
pull-offs/hammer-ons
PO H PO H
PO H PO H
harmonics
SL
m i
p
H
H SL
SL
H
SL
vibrato

vibrato
mute
PO H
H
'punch' strum
'roll' chord
rasqueado
SL
H PO
roll

mute mute mute mute
p i p m p m p i
SL
power strum chords with "p" and "m"
vibrato
p m p i p m p i
power strum "p" then "i"
p i p m p m p i
SL SL SL
p i p i p i p i p m p i
T A B

73
76
muted notes
80
(Slide used in measures 84 - 102)
84
SL
88
1.
SL SL

Tapping begins here. Tap at fret # indicated by square. Non-squared notes are fingered with left hand but still tapped at fret 7.

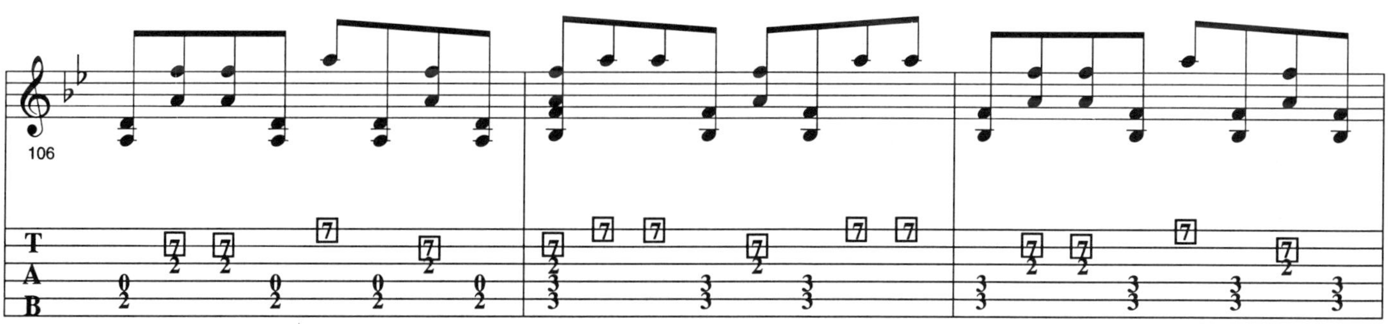

Right hand continues tapping in this fashion; melody with "m", base notes with "i".

Left hand frets at 2.
Right hand taps fret at 14 and 12.
Tap fret 12 open.
Compensate 12 frets below with left hand for squared 15, 16, and 17 tapped frets.

124
127
130
1.
133
2.
137
T
A
B

Acoustic Fingerstyle Workshop Credits

To order additional copies of this book, or for more information about Richard's complete catalog, contact Mel Bay Publications, Inc. or Gillazilla Music; PO Box 3023, Inverness, FL 34451; Phone: 352-860-2422; email: contact@richardgilewitz.com.

Photo Credits: Wayne Brown: Greenbrier Music, Anniston, AL (front cover)
Tim Ward: Masterpiece Productions, Inc. Seattle, WA
Richard Gilewitz
Michael Stock: WLRN, Miami, FL
Gill Winter: Flying Piglets, New Zealand

Illustrations: Hand Chart: Randy Rhea, DDS, Little Rock, AR
Foot in Mouth: Jesse Pyron

Project Coordinator: Beverly Phillips: Alligator Alley Productions, Inverness, FL

Music & Text Editing: DVD Filming: Doug Witherspoon: Mel Bay Publications, Inc.;
Stephen B. Rekas: Mel Bay Publications, Inc.

Special thanks to my most treasured mentors Mr. Ki Chon Choi and David Walbert. To the hundreds of music shops and guitar dealers worldwide who have hosted my clinics — you have made it possible for music to remain alive in you communities. To the following companies who have supported this program throughout my career: Audio-Technica, Breedlove Guitars, L.R. Baggs, D'Addario Strings, Planet Waves, GHS Strings, Peavey Electronics, Sabine Tuners, Shubb Capos, SWR, Tacoma Guitars, Tech 21 and Rivera Amps.

And lastly, to all of the many fans of guitar — this book is for you.

The songs contained in this book can be found on the following recordings:
Voluntary Solitary, Richard Gilewitz, Gillazilla Records
"Mrs. Firecracker's Place"
"Jamaicalina"
"Pre-dawn Mourning"
"The Maison Blanche Exit Song"

Synapse Collapse, Richard Gilewitz, Gillazilla Records
"Echoing Gilewitz" (part of "Echoing Wilderness"), Richard Gilewitz, Gillazilla Records and
A Shout Toward Noon (as Echoing Gilewitz), Leo Kottke, Private Music
"Dirt To Dust"
"Bilingual Fantasy"

Thumbsing, Richard Gilewitz, Gillazilla Records
"Dirt to Dust" with "Gypsy Minor" intro